nickelodeon™

降击神通

AVATAR

THE LAST AIRBENDER™

Created by
Bryan Konietzko
Michael Dante DiMartino

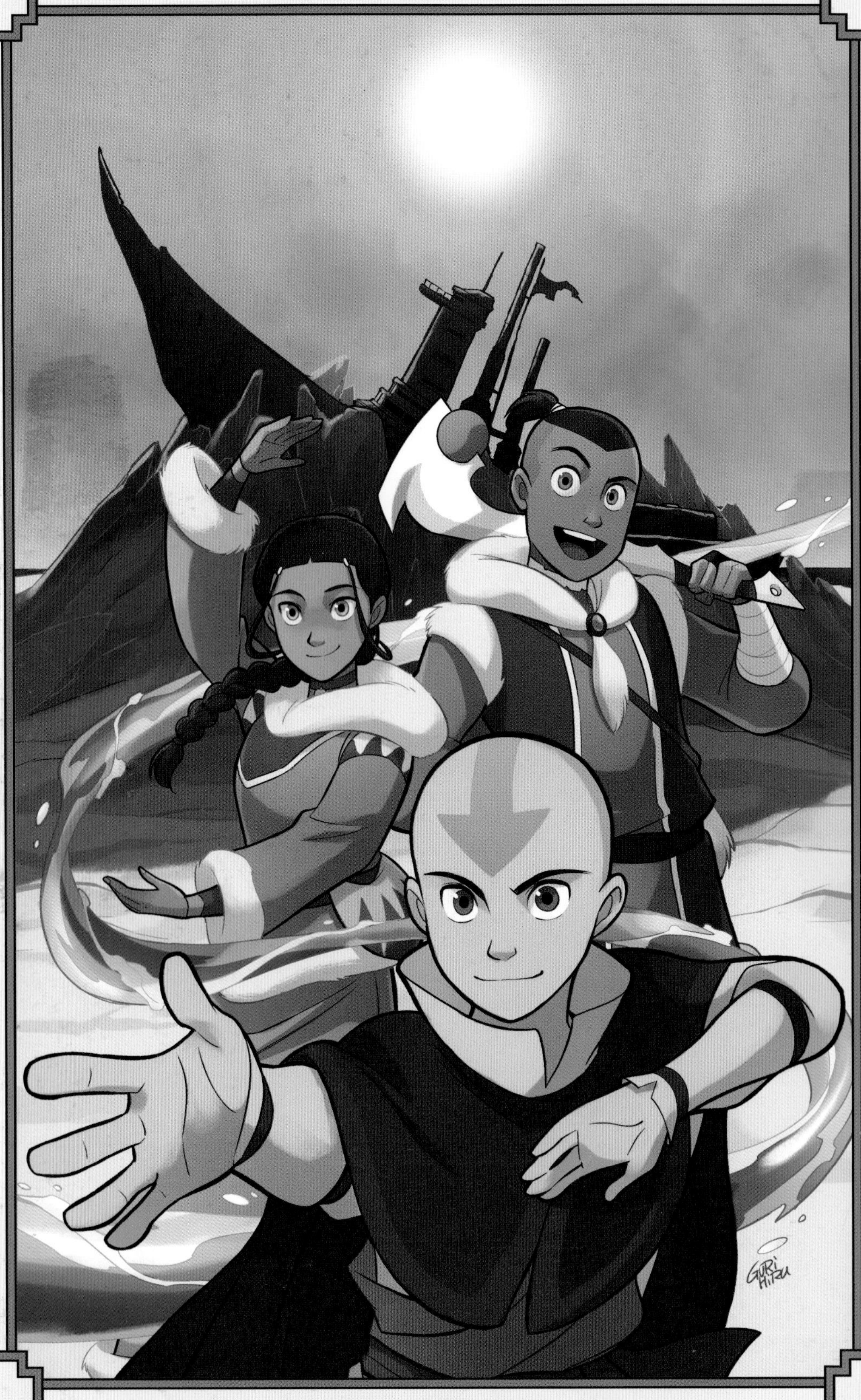
GURI HIRU

nickelodeon™

降击神通

AVATAR

THE LAST AIRBENDER™

NORTH AND SOUTH · PART ONE

script
GENE LUEN YANG

art and cover
GURIHIRU

lettering
MICHAEL HEISLER

DARK HORSE BOOKS

president and publisher
MIKE RICHARDSON

editor
DAVE MARSHALL

assistant editor
RACHEL ROBERTS

collection designer
SARAH TERRY

digital art technician
CHRISTIANNE GOUDREAU

Special thanks to Linda Lee, Kat van Dam, James Salerno, and Joan Hilty
at Nickelodeon, and to Bryan Konietzko and Michael Dante DiMartino.

Published by **Dark Horse Books**
A division of Dark Horse Comics, Inc.
10956 SE Main Street, Milwaukie, OR 97222

DarkHorse.com
Nick.com

International Licensing: (503) 905-2377
Comic Shop Locator Service: (888) 266-4226

First edition: September 2016| ISBN 978-1-50670-022-9

3 5 7 9 10 8 6 4 2
Printed in China

Neil Hankerson, Executive Vice President • Tom Weddle, Chief Financial Officer • Randy Stradley, Vice President of Publishing • Michael Martens, Vice President of Book Trade Sales • Matt Parkinson, Vice President of Marketing • David Scroggy, Vice President of Product Development • Dale LaFountain, Vice President of Information Technology • Cara Niece, Vice President of Production and Scheduling Nick McWhorter, Vice President of Media Licensing • Ken Lizzi, General Counsel • Dave Marshall, Editor in Chief • Davey Estrada, Editorial Director • Scott Allie, Executive Senior Editor • Chris Warner, Senior Books Editor • Cary Grazzini, Director of Print and Development • Lia Ribacchi, Art Director • Mark Bernardi, Director of Digital Publishing • Michael Gombos, Director of International Publishing and Licensing

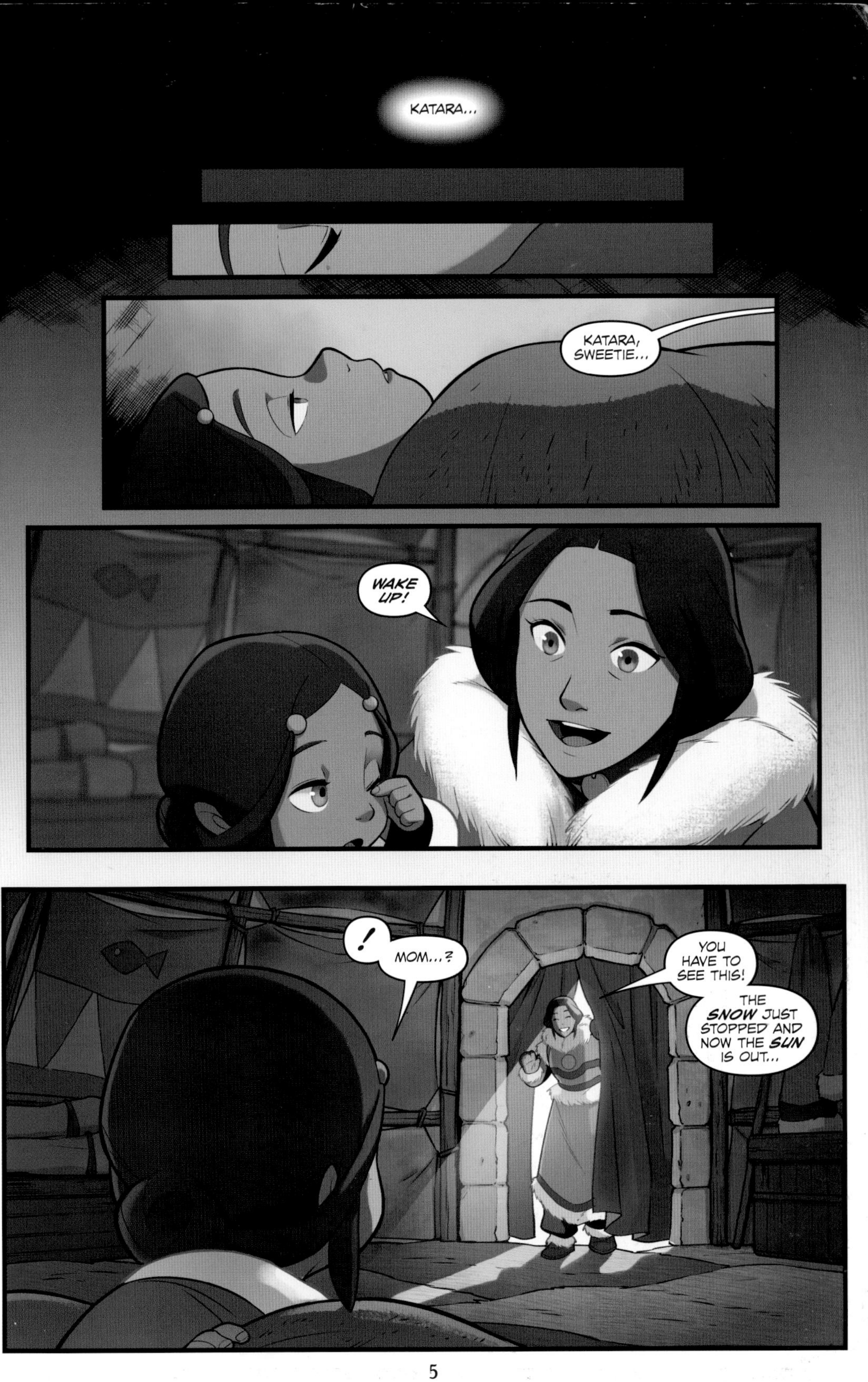
KATARA...
KATARA, SWEETIE...
WAKE UP!
!
MOM...?
YOU HAVE TO SEE THIS!
THE SNOW JUST STOPPED AND NOW THE SUN IS OUT...

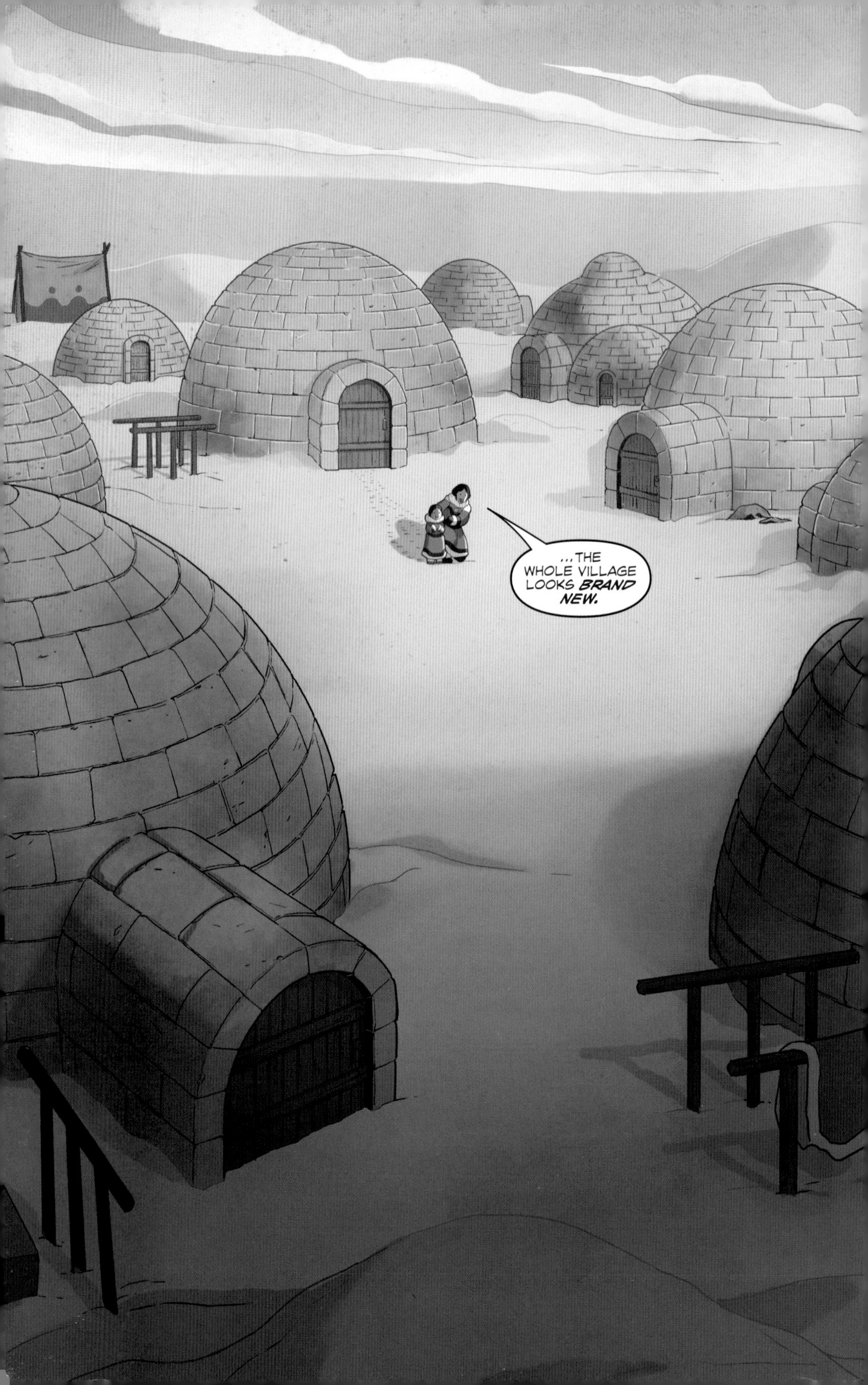
...THE WHOLE VILLAGE LOOKS BRAND NEW.

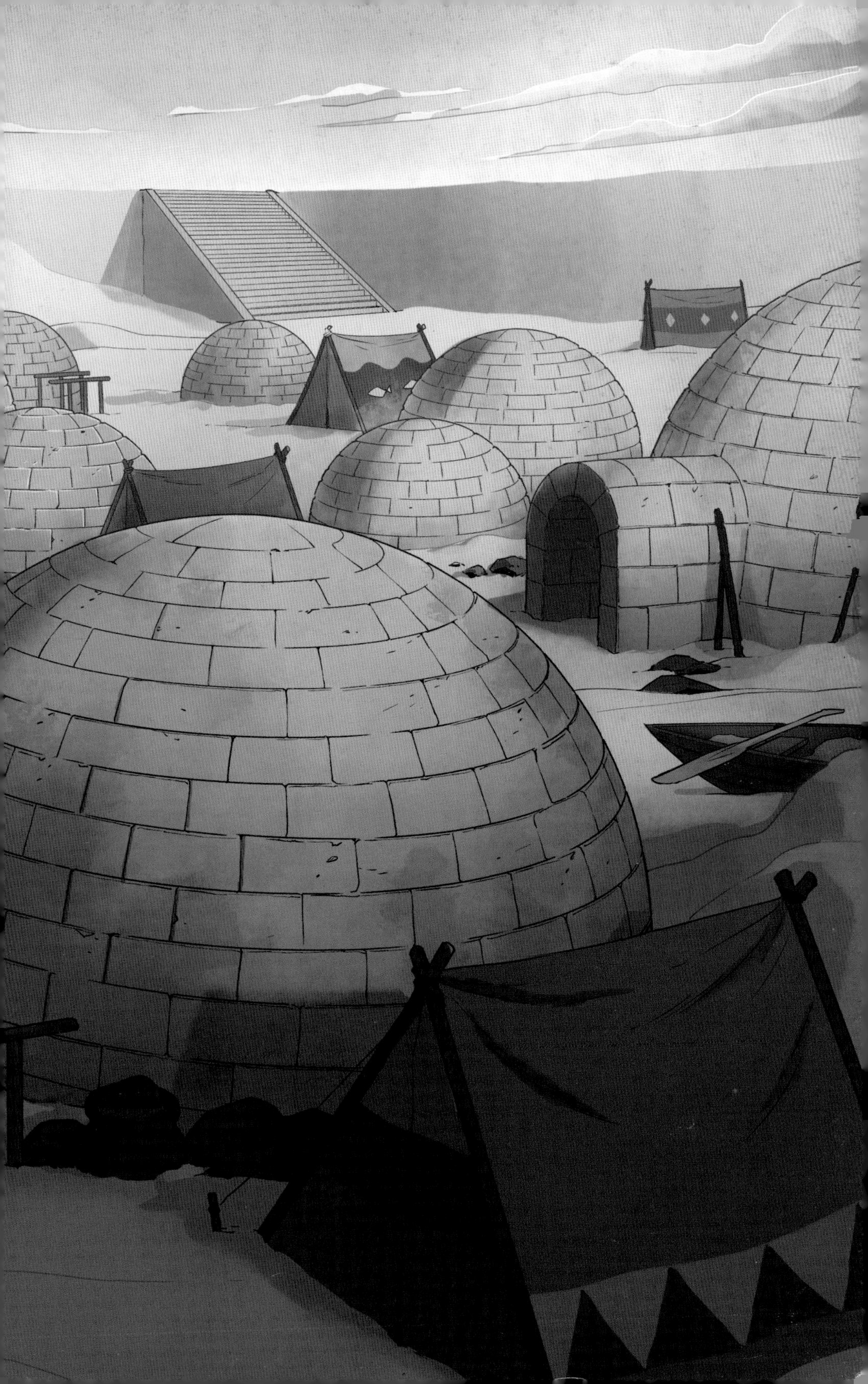

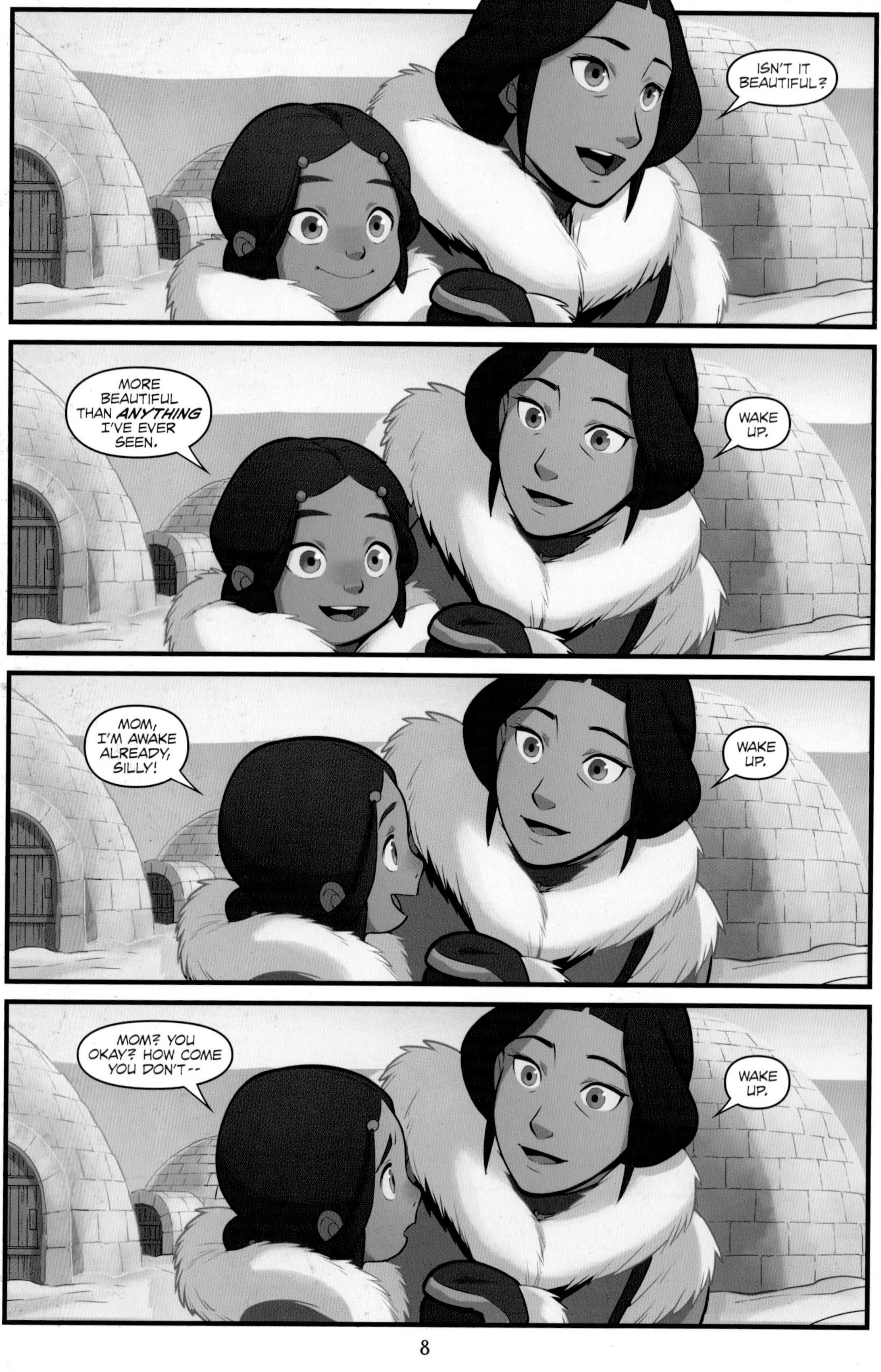
ISN'T IT BEAUTIFUL?
MORE BEAUTIFUL THAN *ANYTHING* I'VE EVER SEEN.
WAKE UP.
MOM, I'M AWAKE ALREADY, SILLY!
WAKE UP.
MOM? YOU OKAY? HOW COME YOU DON'T--
WAKE UP.

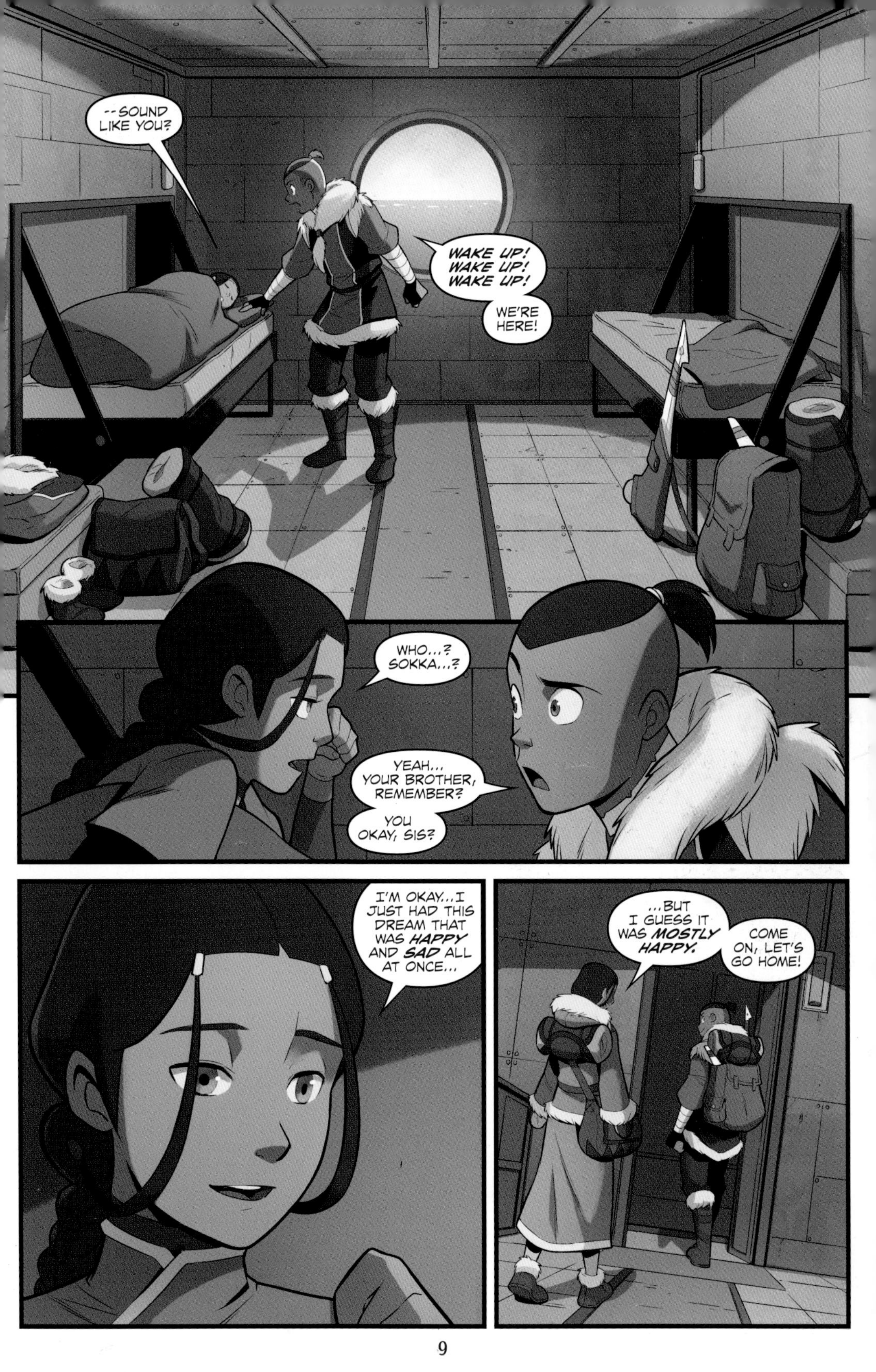
--SOUND LIKE YOU?
WAKE UP! WAKE UP! WAKE UP!
WE'RE HERE!
WHO...? SOKKA...?
YEAH... YOUR BROTHER, REMEMBER?
YOU OKAY, SIS?
I'M OKAY...I JUST HAD THIS DREAM THAT WAS HAPPY AND SAD ALL AT ONCE...
...BUT I GUESS IT WAS MOSTLY HAPPY.
COME ON, LET'S GO HOME!

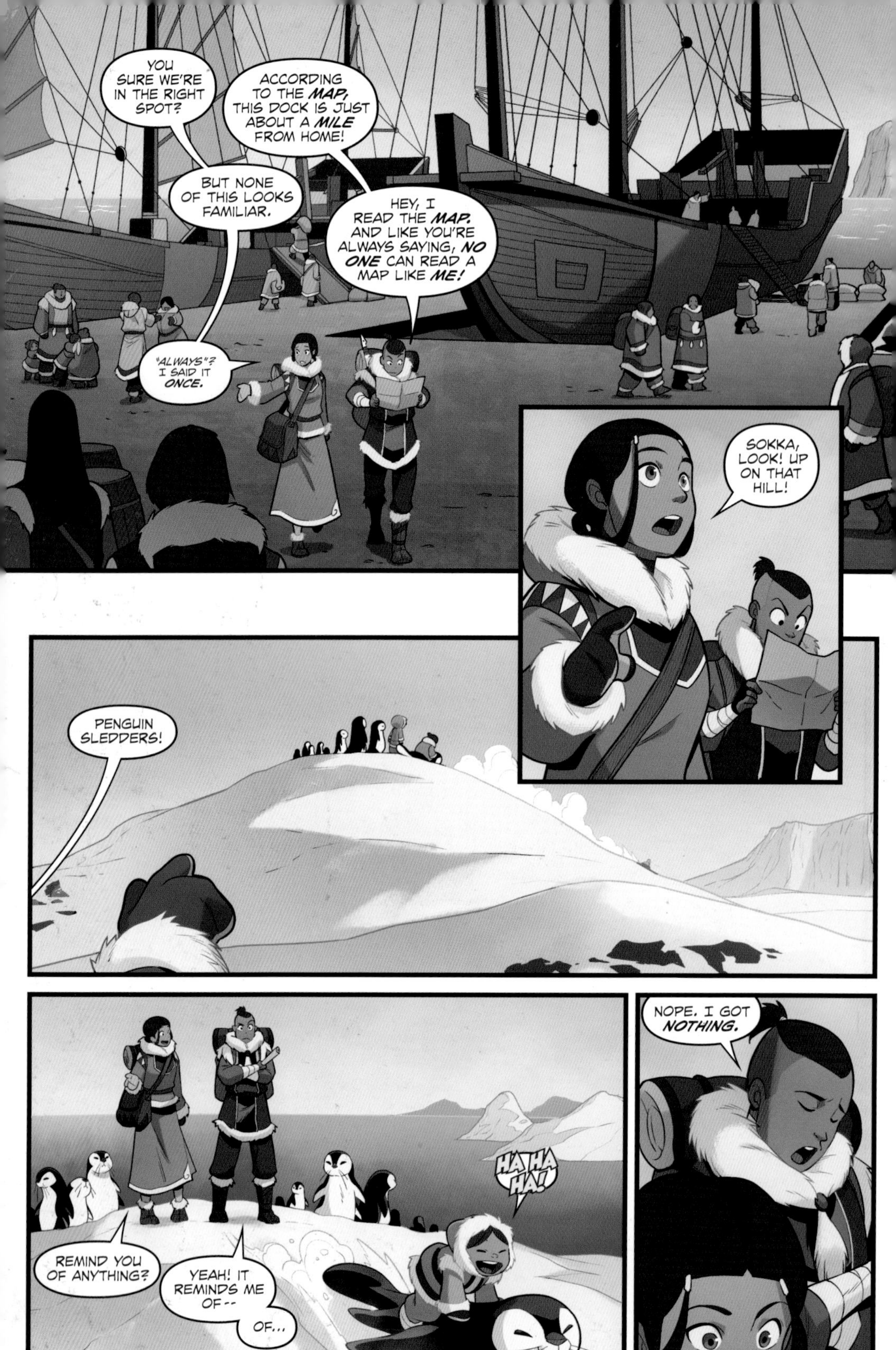
YOU SURE WE'RE IN THE RIGHT SPOT?
ACCORDING TO THE *MAP,* THIS DOCK IS JUST ABOUT A *MILE* FROM HOME!
BUT NONE OF THIS LOOKS FAMILIAR.
HEY, I READ THE *MAP.* AND LIKE YOU'RE ALWAYS SAYING, *NO ONE* CAN READ A MAP LIKE *ME!*
"ALWAYS"? I SAID IT *ONCE.*
SOKKA, LOOK! UP ON THAT HILL!
PENGUIN SLEDDERS!
REMIND YOU OF ANYTHING?
YEAH! IT REMINDS ME OF--
OF...
HA HA HA!
NOPE. I GOT *NOTHING.*

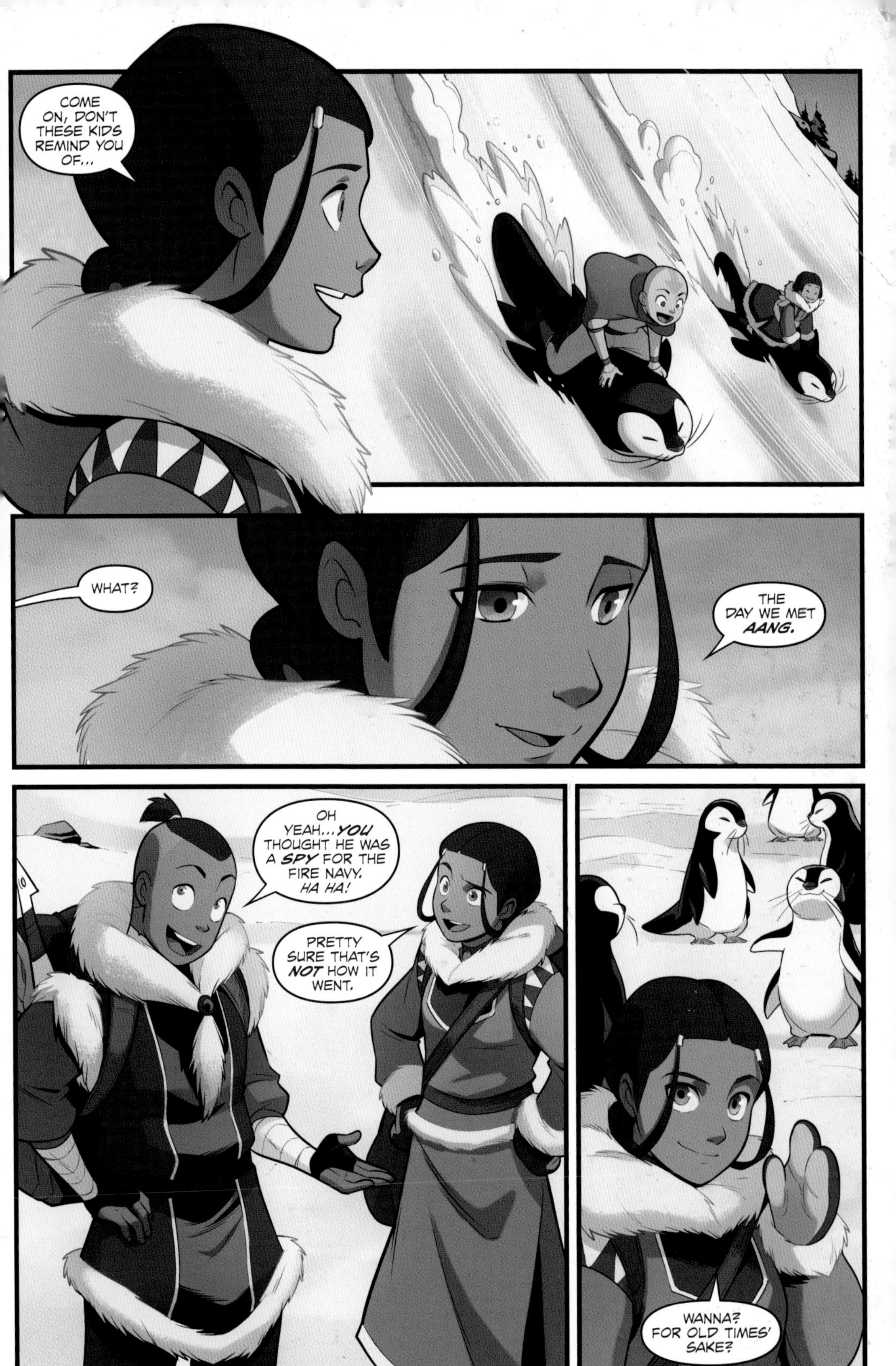
COME ON, DON'T THESE KIDS REMIND YOU OF...
WHAT?
THE DAY WE MET AANG.
OH YEAH... YOU THOUGHT HE WAS A SPY FOR THE FIRE NAVY. HA HA!
PRETTY SURE THAT'S NOT HOW IT WENT.
WANNA? FOR OLD TIMES' SAKE?

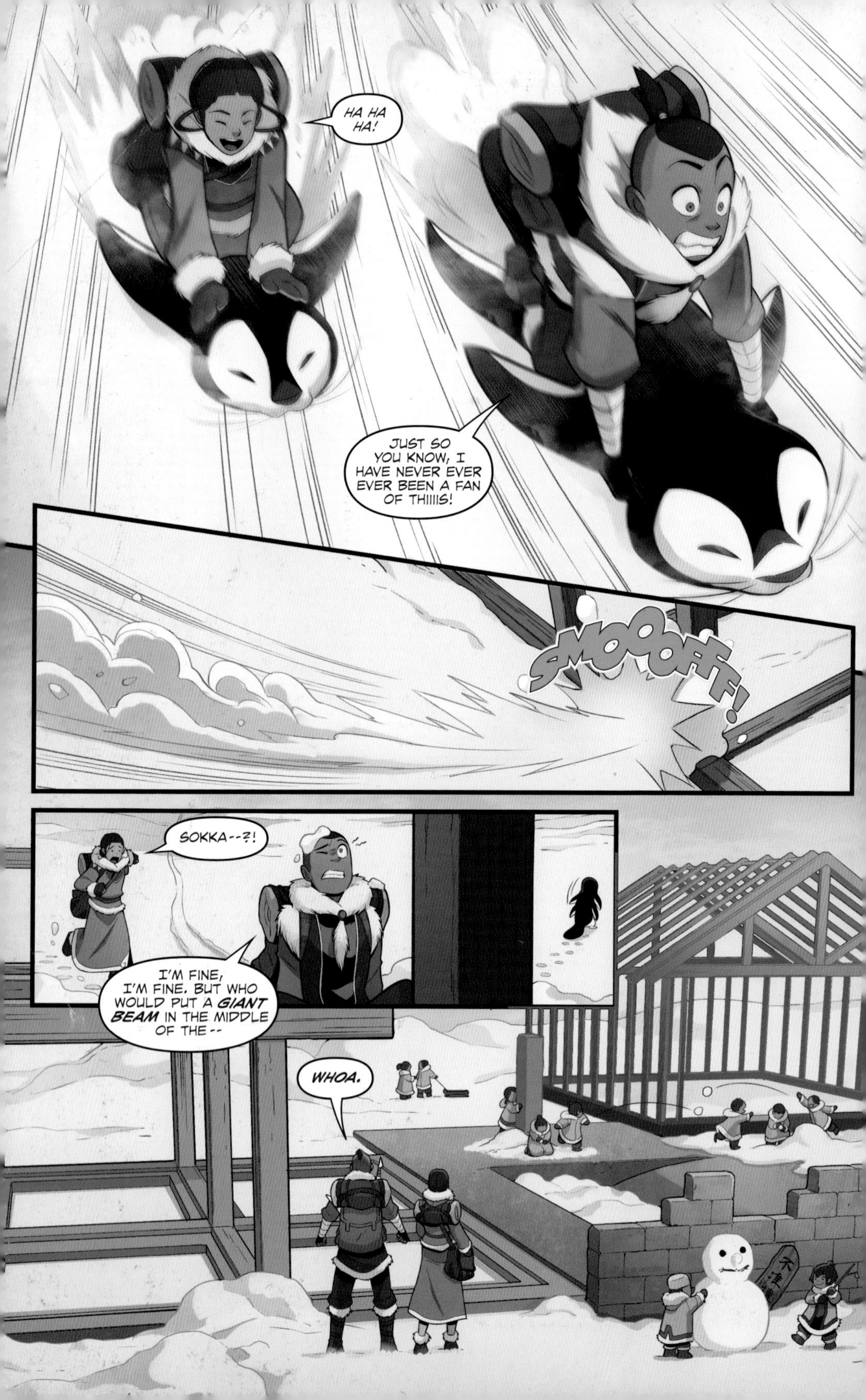
HA HA HA!
JUST SO YOU KNOW, I HAVE NEVER EVER EVER BEEN A FAN OF THIIIIS!
SMOOOFFF!
SOKKA--?!
I'M FINE, I'M FINE. BUT WHO WOULD PUT A GIANT BEAM IN THE MIDDLE OF THE --
WHOA.

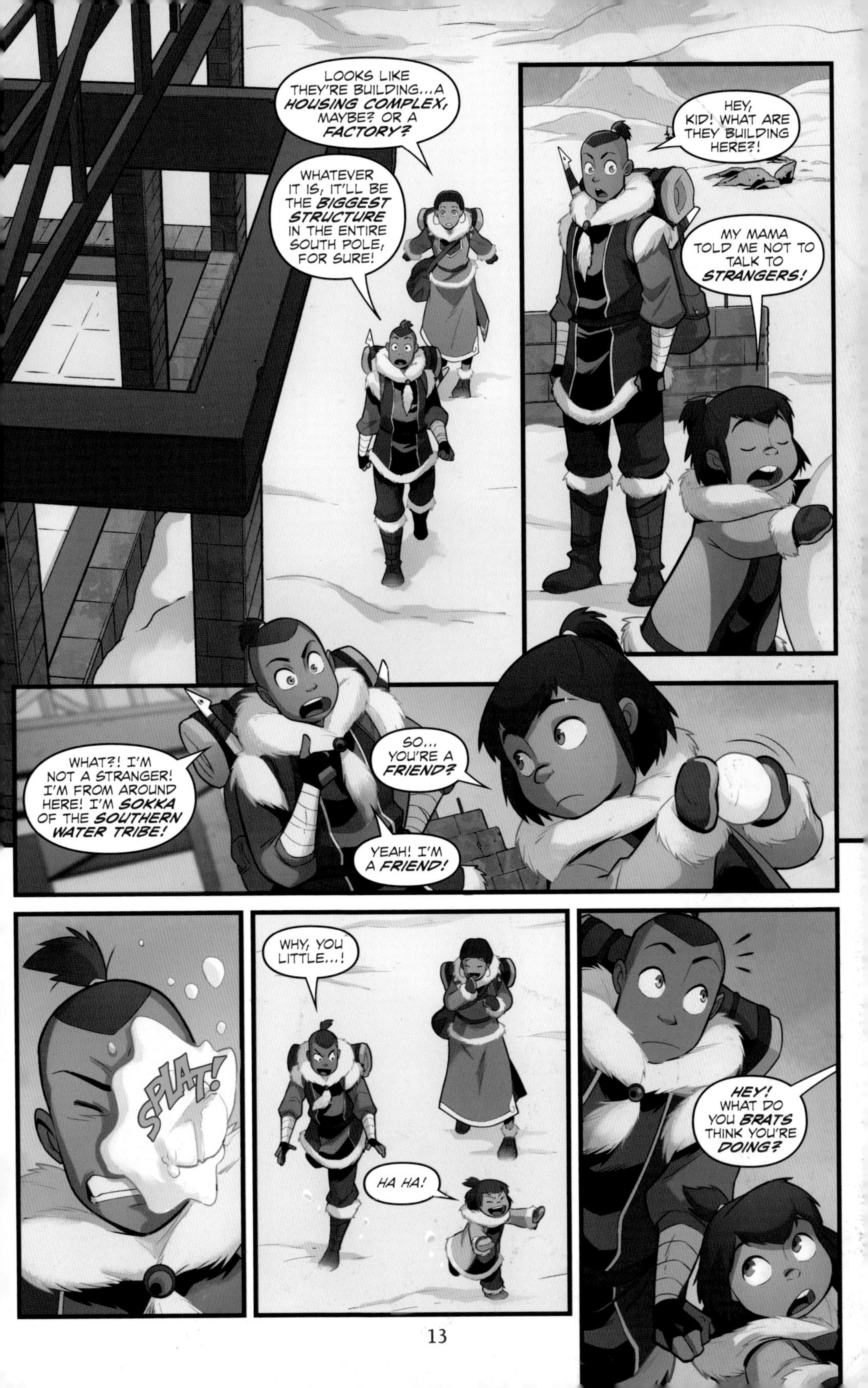
LOOKS LIKE THEY'RE BUILDING...A HOUSING COMPLEX, MAYBE? OR A FACTORY?
WHATEVER IT IS, IT'LL BE THE BIGGEST STRUCTURE IN THE ENTIRE SOUTH POLE, FOR SURE!
HEY, KID! WHAT ARE THEY BUILDING HERE?!
MY MAMA TOLD ME NOT TO TALK TO STRANGERS!
WHAT?! I'M NOT A STRANGER! I'M FROM AROUND HERE! I'M SOKKA OF THE SOUTHERN WATER TRIBE!
SO... YOU'RE A FRIEND?
YEAH! I'M A FRIEND!
SPLAT!
WHY, YOU LITTLE...!
HA HA!
HEY! WHAT DO YOU BRATS THINK YOU'RE DOING?

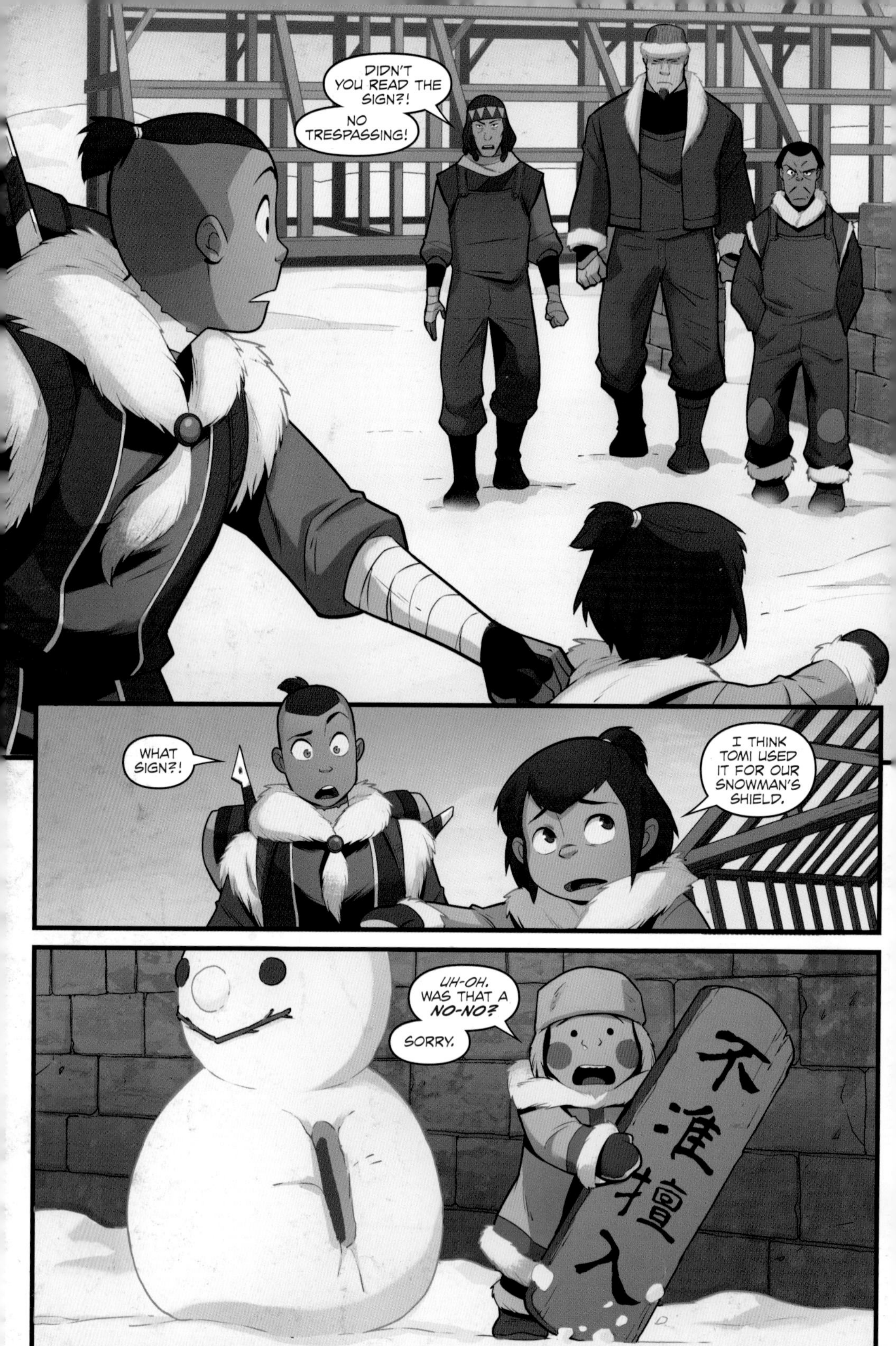
DIDN'T YOU READ THE SIGN?!
NO TRESPASSING!
WHAT SIGN?!
I THINK TOMI USED IT FOR OUR SNOWMAN'S SHIELD.
UH-OH. WAS THAT A *NO-NO?*
SORRY.
不准擅入

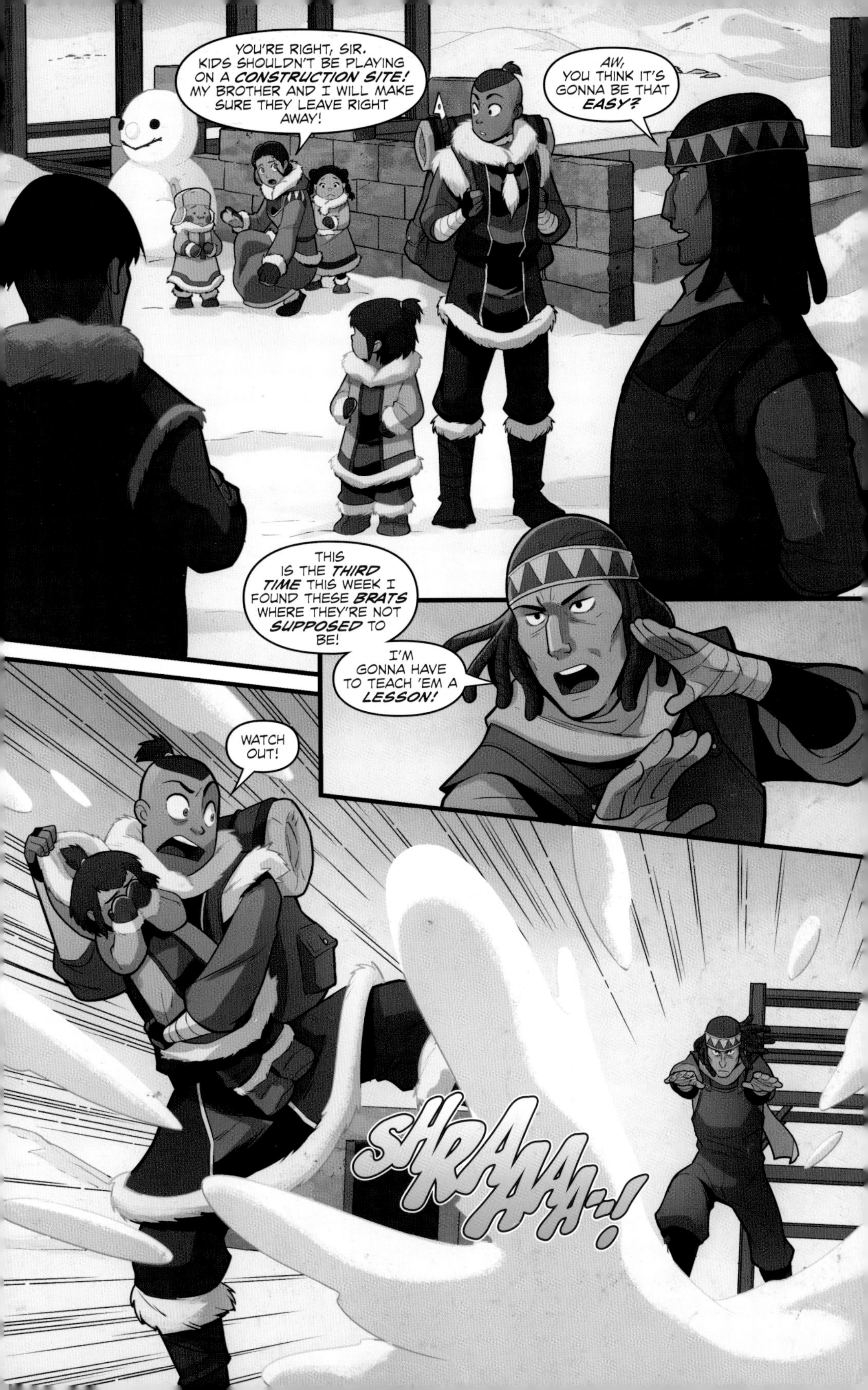
YOU'RE RIGHT, SIR. KIDS SHOULDN'T BE PLAYING ON A CONSTRUCTION SITE! MY BROTHER AND I WILL MAKE SURE THEY LEAVE RIGHT AWAY!
AW, YOU THINK IT'S GONNA BE THAT EASY?
THIS IS THE THIRD TIME THIS WEEK I FOUND THESE BRATS WHERE THEY'RE NOT SUPPOSED TO BE!
I'M GONNA HAVE TO TEACH 'EM A LESSON!
WATCH OUT!
SHRAAAA--!

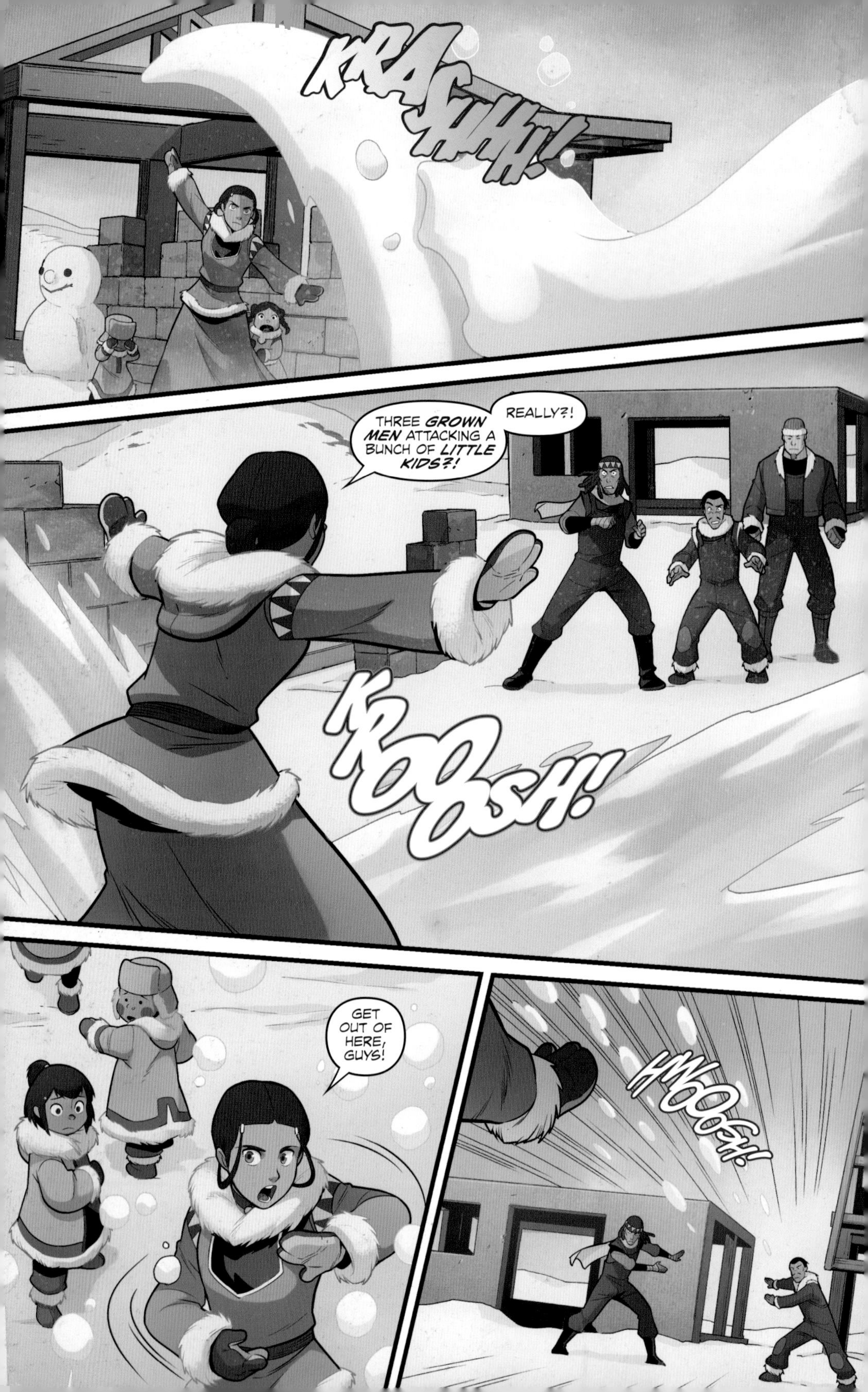
KRASHHH!
THREE GROWN MEN ATTACKING A BUNCH OF LITTLE KIDS?!
REALLY?!
KROOOSH!
GET OUT OF HERE, GUYS!
HWOOOSH!

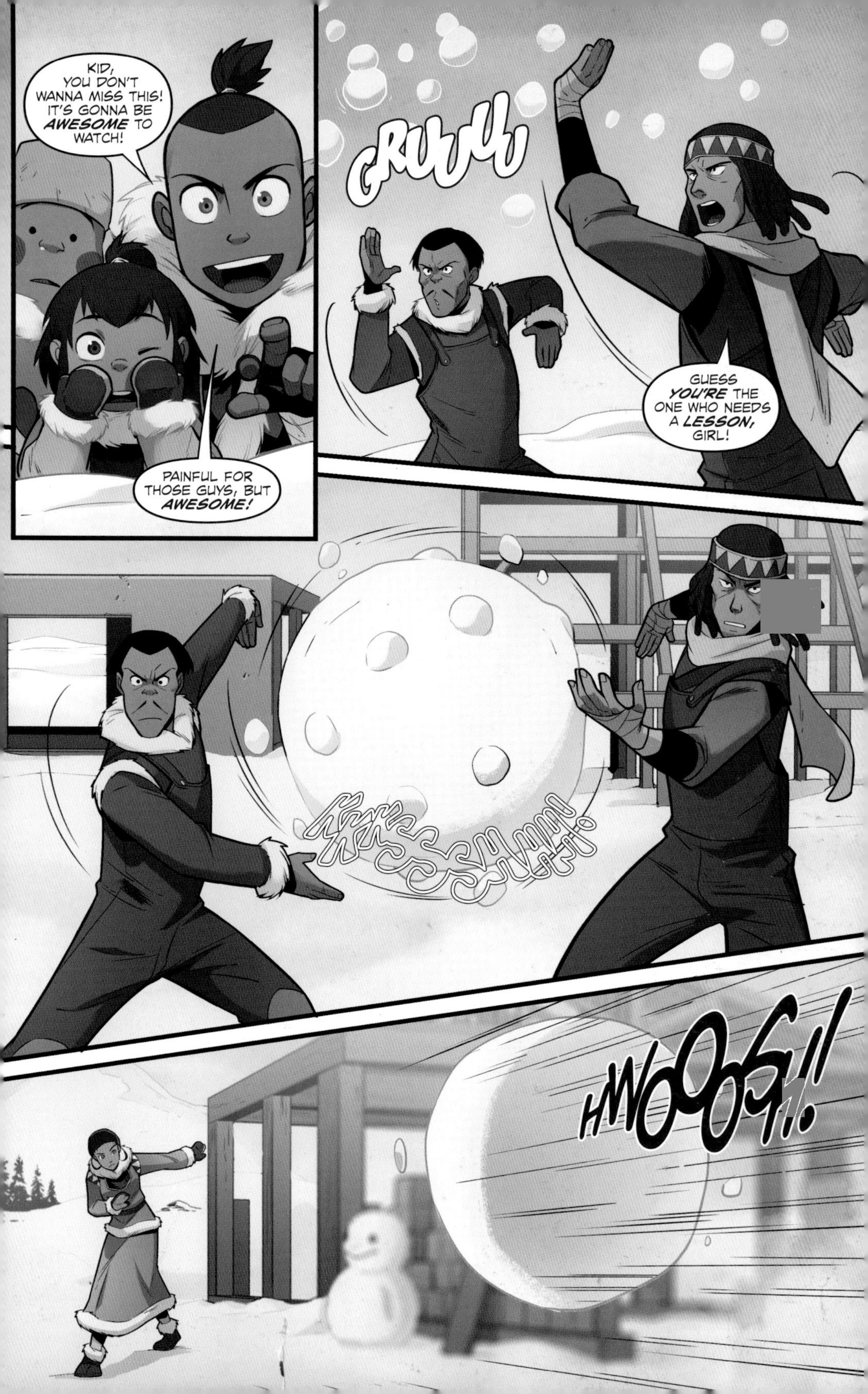
KID, YOU DON'T WANNA MISS THIS! IT'S GONNA BE **AWESOME** TO WATCH!
PAINFUL FOR THOSE GUYS, BUT **AWESOME!**
GRUUU
GUESS **YOU'RE** THE ONE WHO NEEDS A **LESSON,** GIRL!
HWOOOSH!!

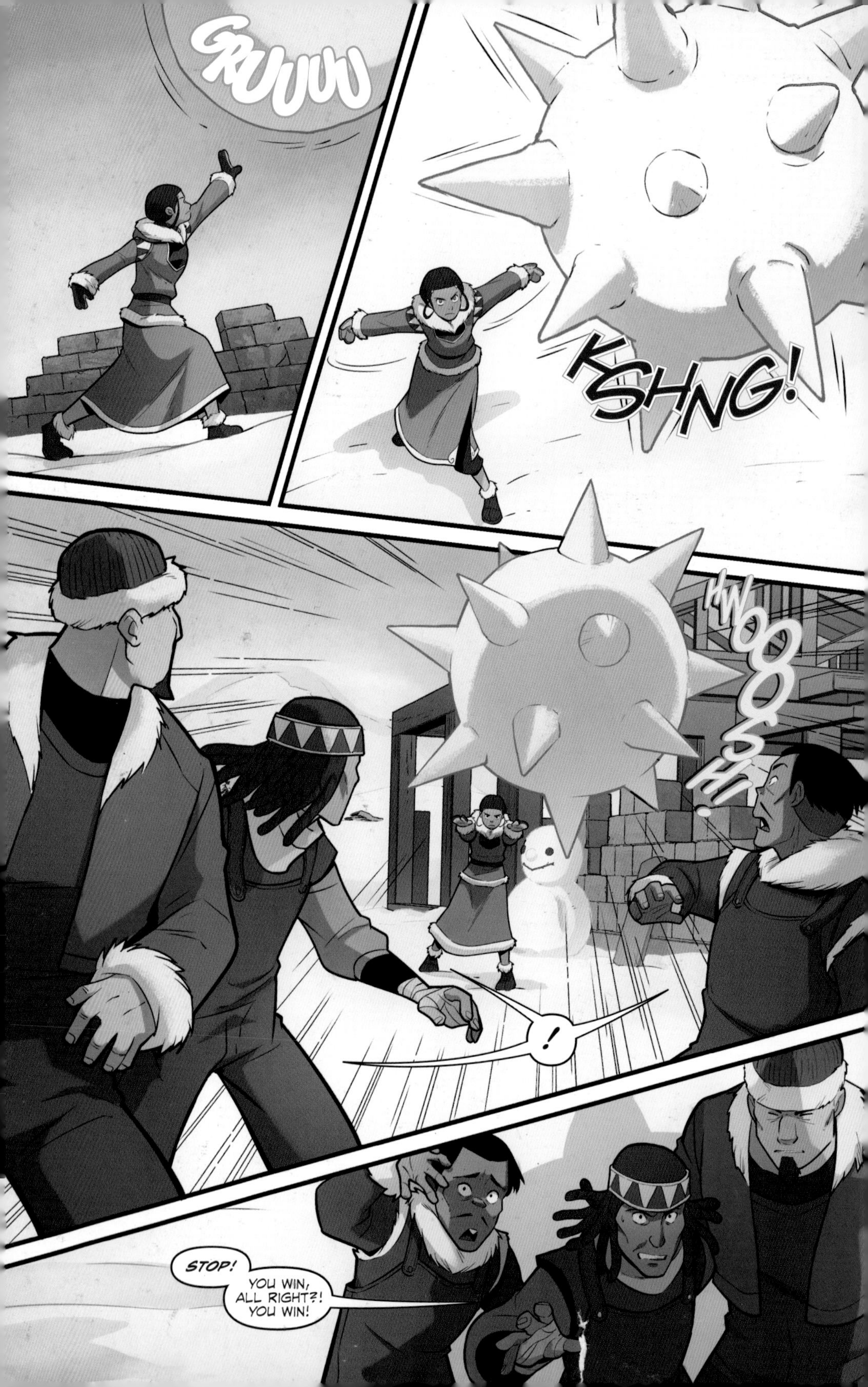
GRUUUU
KSHNG!
HWOOOOSH!!
!
STOP!
YOU WIN, ALL RIGHT?! YOU WIN!

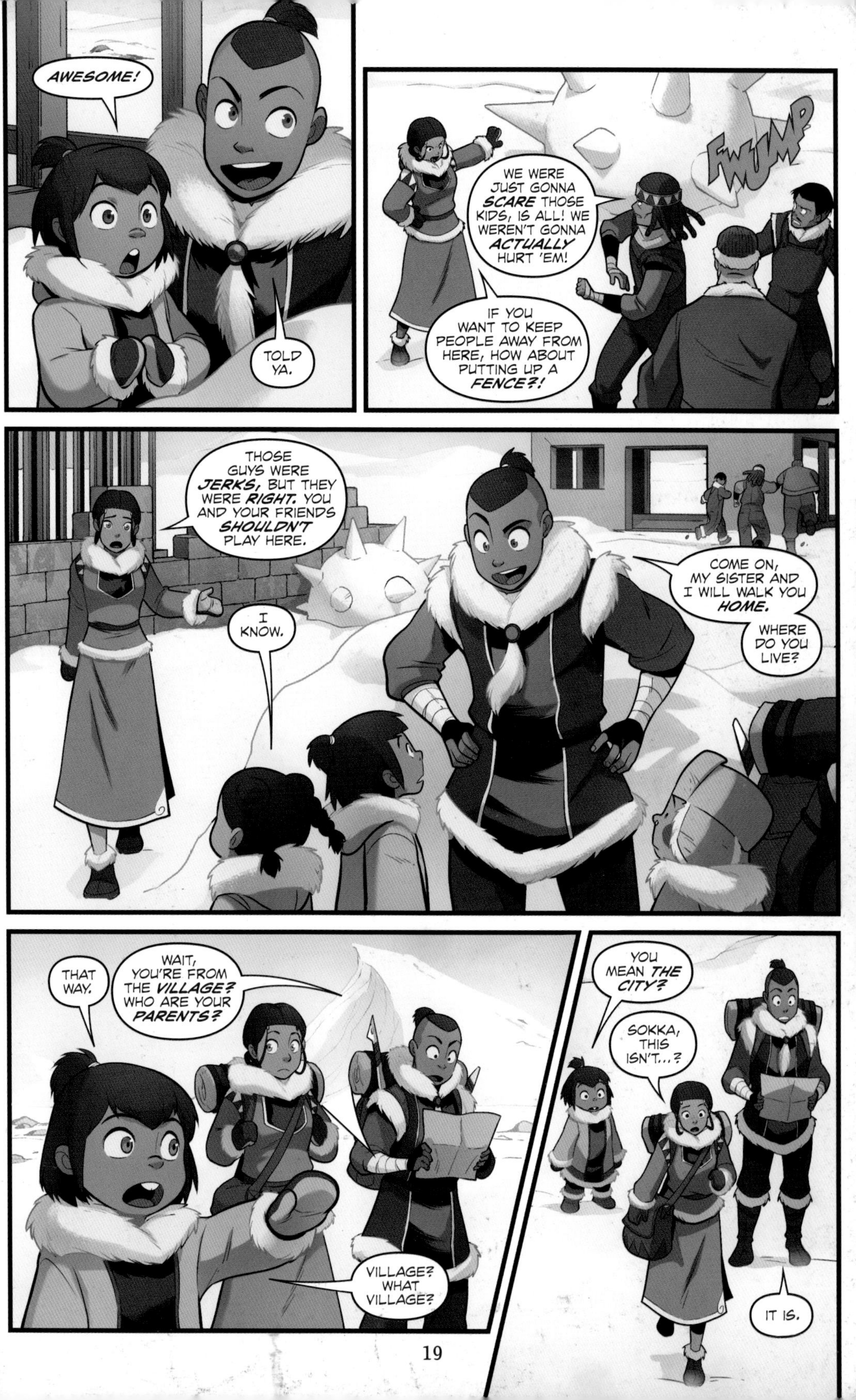
AWESOME!
TOLD YA.
WE WERE JUST GONNA SCARE THOSE KIDS, IS ALL! WE WEREN'T GONNA ACTUALLY HURT 'EM!
FWUMP
IF YOU WANT TO KEEP PEOPLE AWAY FROM HERE, HOW ABOUT PUTTING UP A FENCE?!
THOSE GUYS WERE JERKS, BUT THEY WERE RIGHT. YOU AND YOUR FRIENDS SHOULDN'T PLAY HERE.
I KNOW.
COME ON, MY SISTER AND I WILL WALK YOU HOME.
WHERE DO YOU LIVE?
THAT WAY.
WAIT, YOU'RE FROM THE VILLAGE? WHO ARE YOUR PARENTS?
VILLAGE? WHAT VILLAGE?
YOU MEAN THE CITY?
SOKKA, THIS ISN'T...?
IT IS.

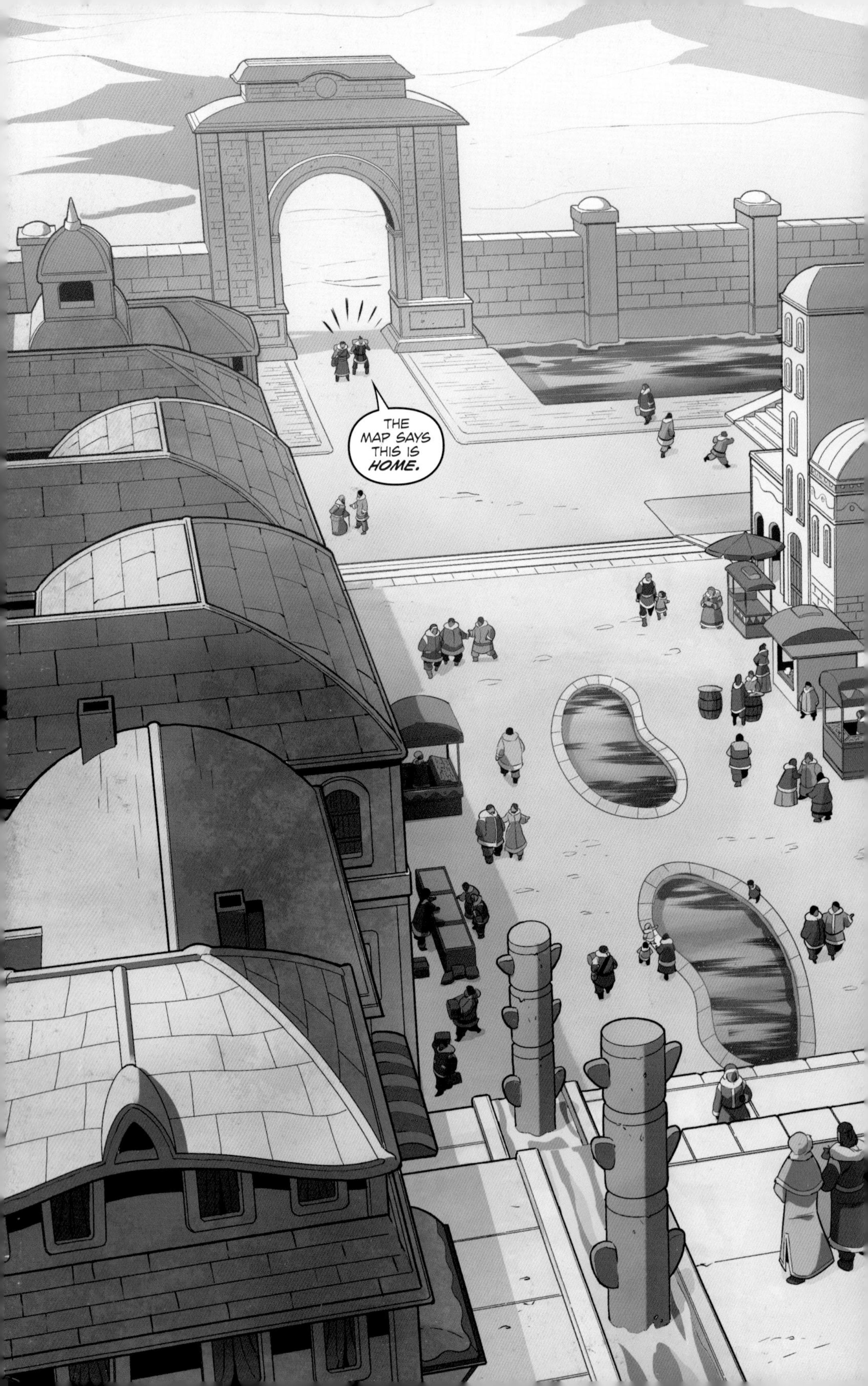
THE MAP SAYS THIS IS *HOME.*

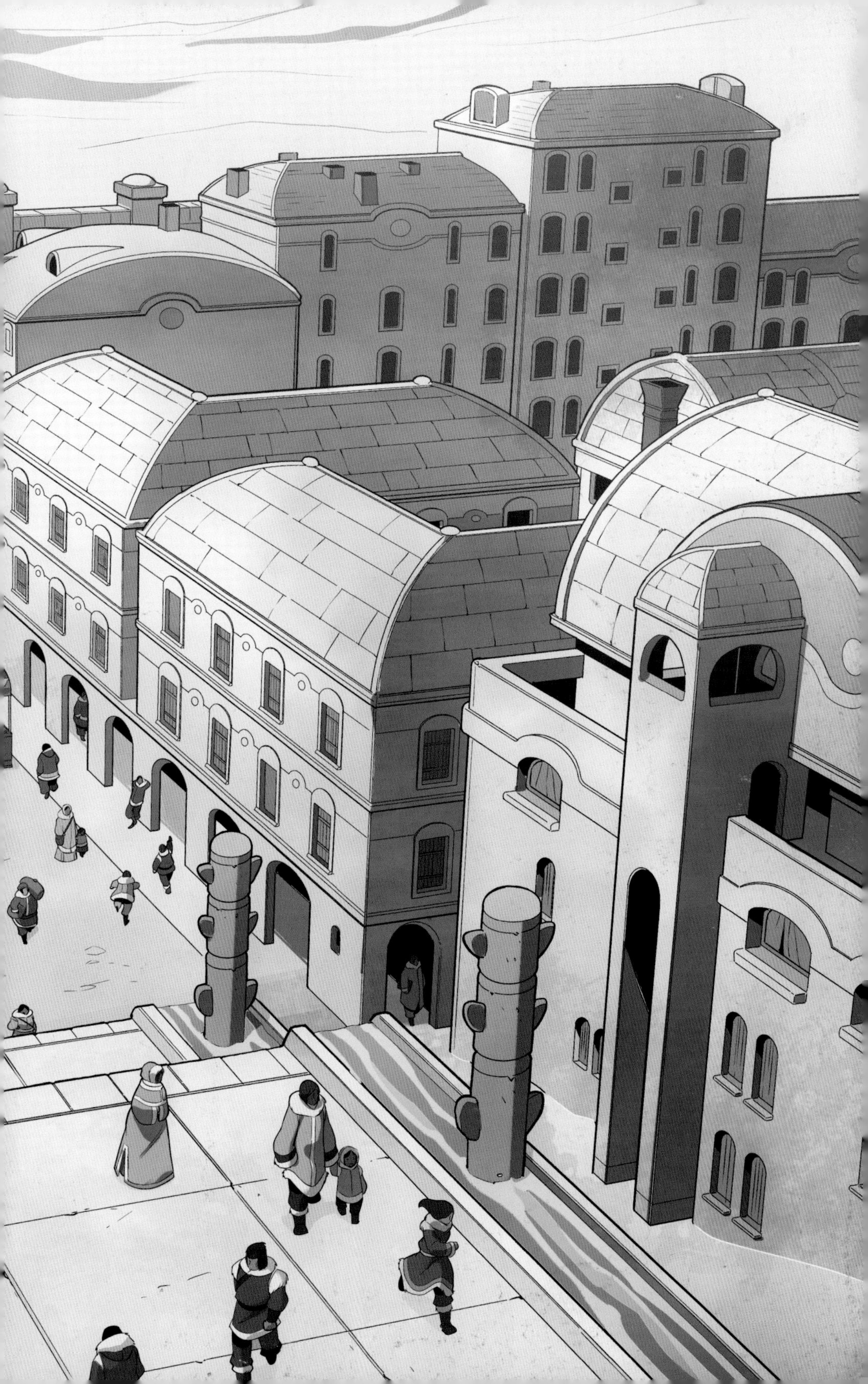

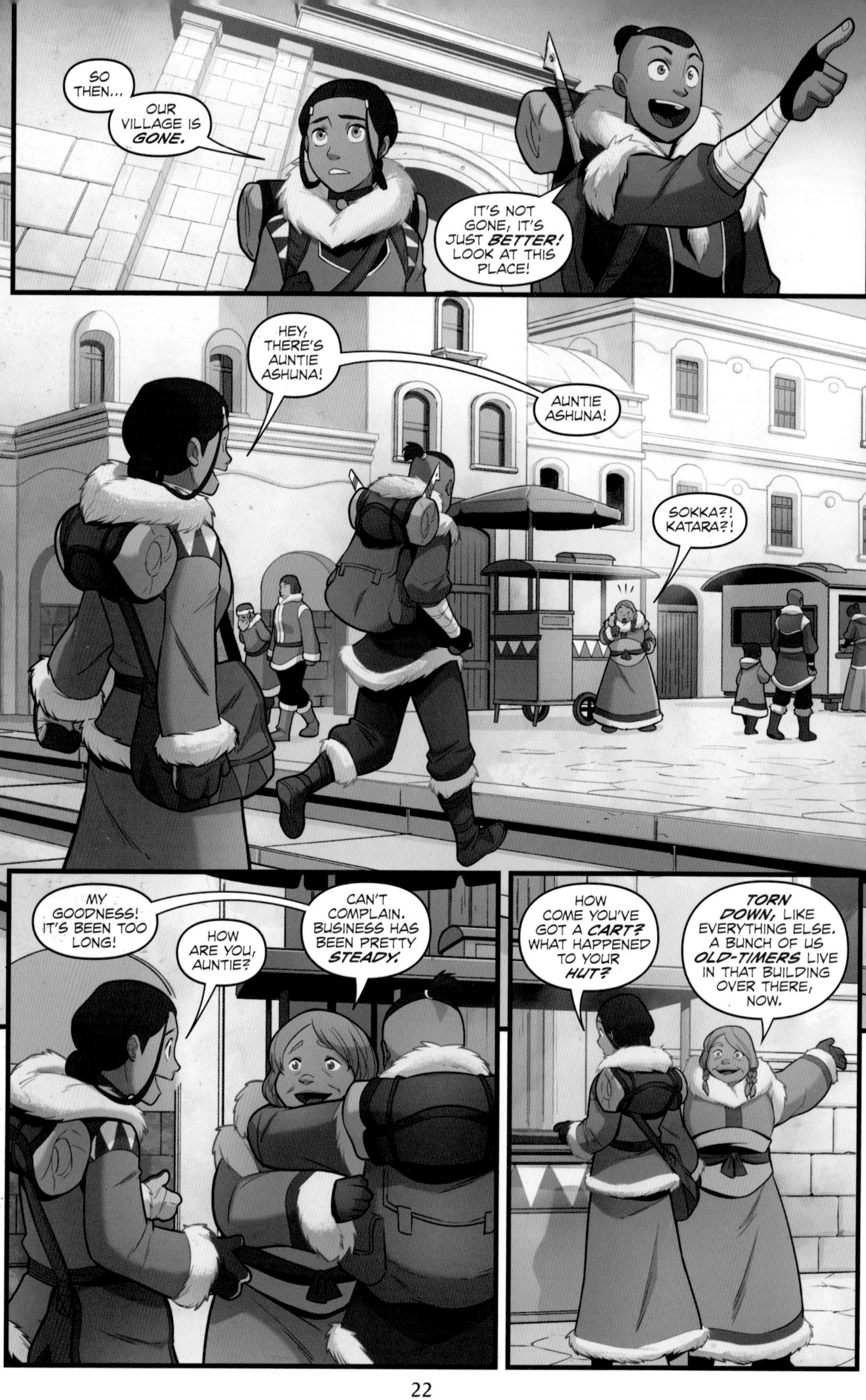
SO THEN...
OUR VILLAGE IS GONE.
IT'S NOT GONE, IT'S JUST BETTER! LOOK AT THIS PLACE!
HEY, THERE'S AUNTIE ASHUNA!
AUNTIE ASHUNA!
SOKKA?! KATARA?!
MY GOODNESS! IT'S BEEN TOO LONG!
HOW ARE YOU, AUNTIE?
CAN'T COMPLAIN. BUSINESS HAS BEEN PRETTY STEADY.
HOW COME YOU'VE GOT A CART? WHAT HAPPENED TO YOUR HUT?
TORN DOWN, LIKE EVERYTHING ELSE. A BUNCH OF US OLD-TIMERS LIVE IN THAT BUILDING OVER THERE, NOW.

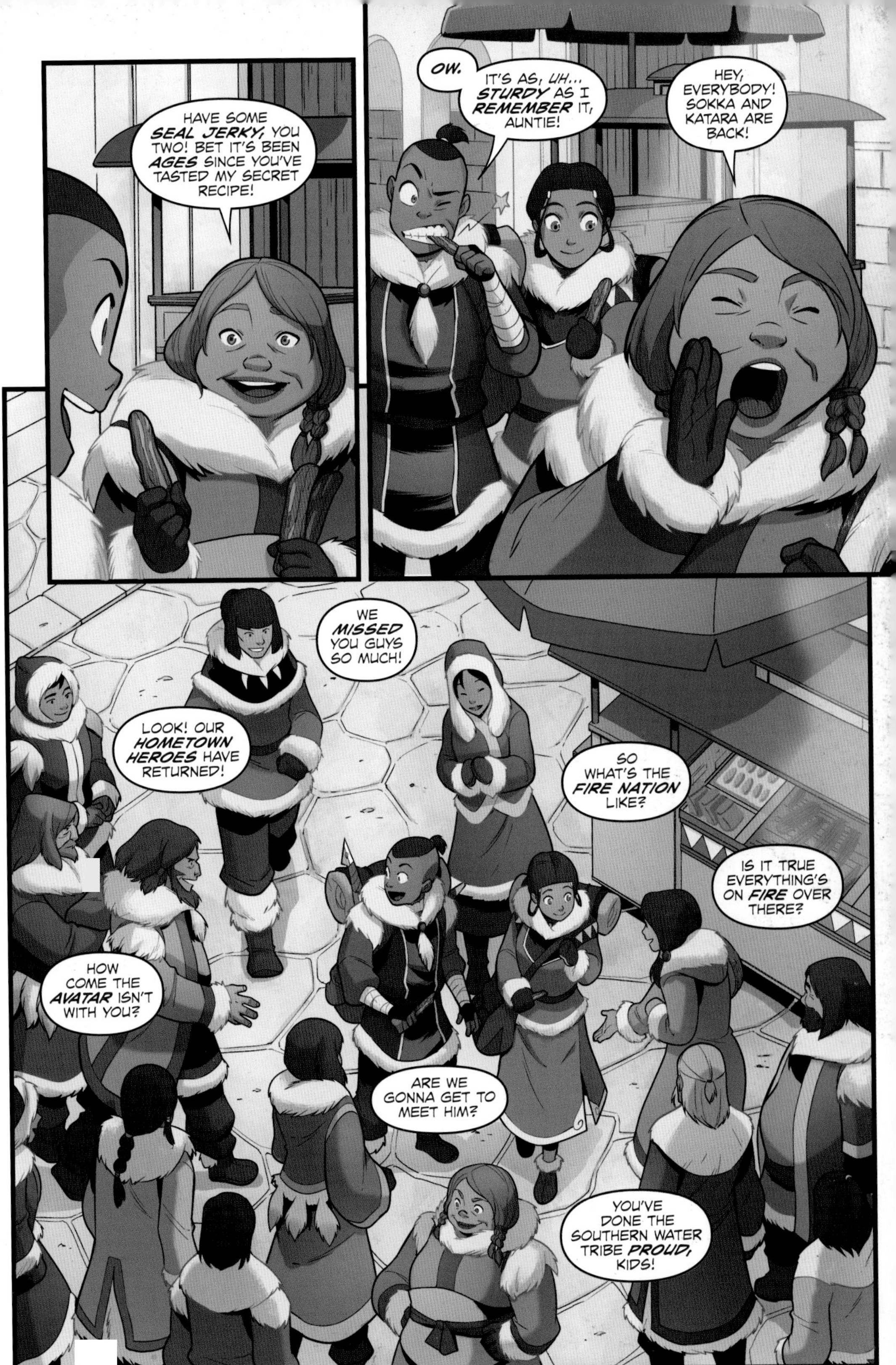
HAVE SOME SEAL JERKY, YOU TWO! BET IT'S BEEN AGES SINCE YOU'VE TASTED MY SECRET RECIPE!
OW.
IT'S AS, UH... STURDY AS I REMEMBER IT, AUNTIE!
HEY, EVERYBODY! SOKKA AND KATARA ARE BACK!
WE MISSED YOU GUYS SO MUCH!
LOOK! OUR HOMETOWN HEROES HAVE RETURNED!
SO WHAT'S THE FIRE NATION LIKE?
IS IT TRUE EVERYTHING'S ON FIRE OVER THERE?
HOW COME THE AVATAR ISN'T WITH YOU?
ARE WE GONNA GET TO MEET HIM?
YOU'VE DONE THE SOUTHERN WATER TRIBE PROUD, KIDS!

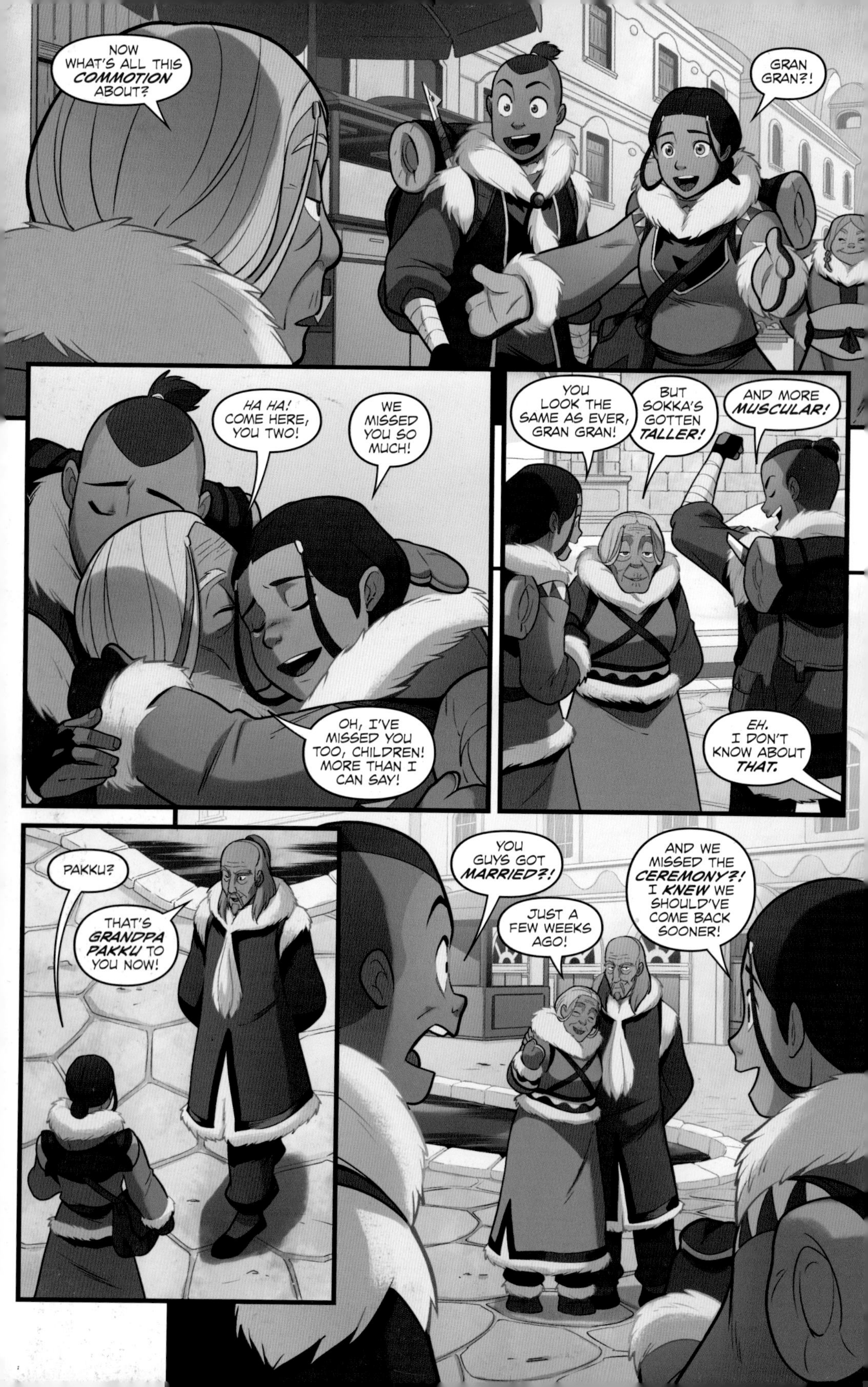
NOW WHAT'S ALL THIS *COMMOTION* ABOUT?
GRAN GRAN?!
HA HA! COME HERE, YOU TWO!
WE MISSED YOU SO MUCH!
OH, I'VE MISSED YOU TOO, CHILDREN! MORE THAN I CAN SAY!
YOU LOOK THE SAME AS EVER, GRAN GRAN!
BUT SOKKA'S GOTTEN *TALLER!*
AND MORE *MUSCULAR!*
EH. I DON'T KNOW ABOUT *THAT.*
PAKKU?
THAT'S *GRANDPA PAKKU* TO YOU NOW!
YOU GUYS GOT *MARRIED?!*
JUST A FEW WEEKS AGO!
AND WE MISSED THE *CEREMONY?!* I *KNEW* WE SHOULD'VE COME BACK SOONER!

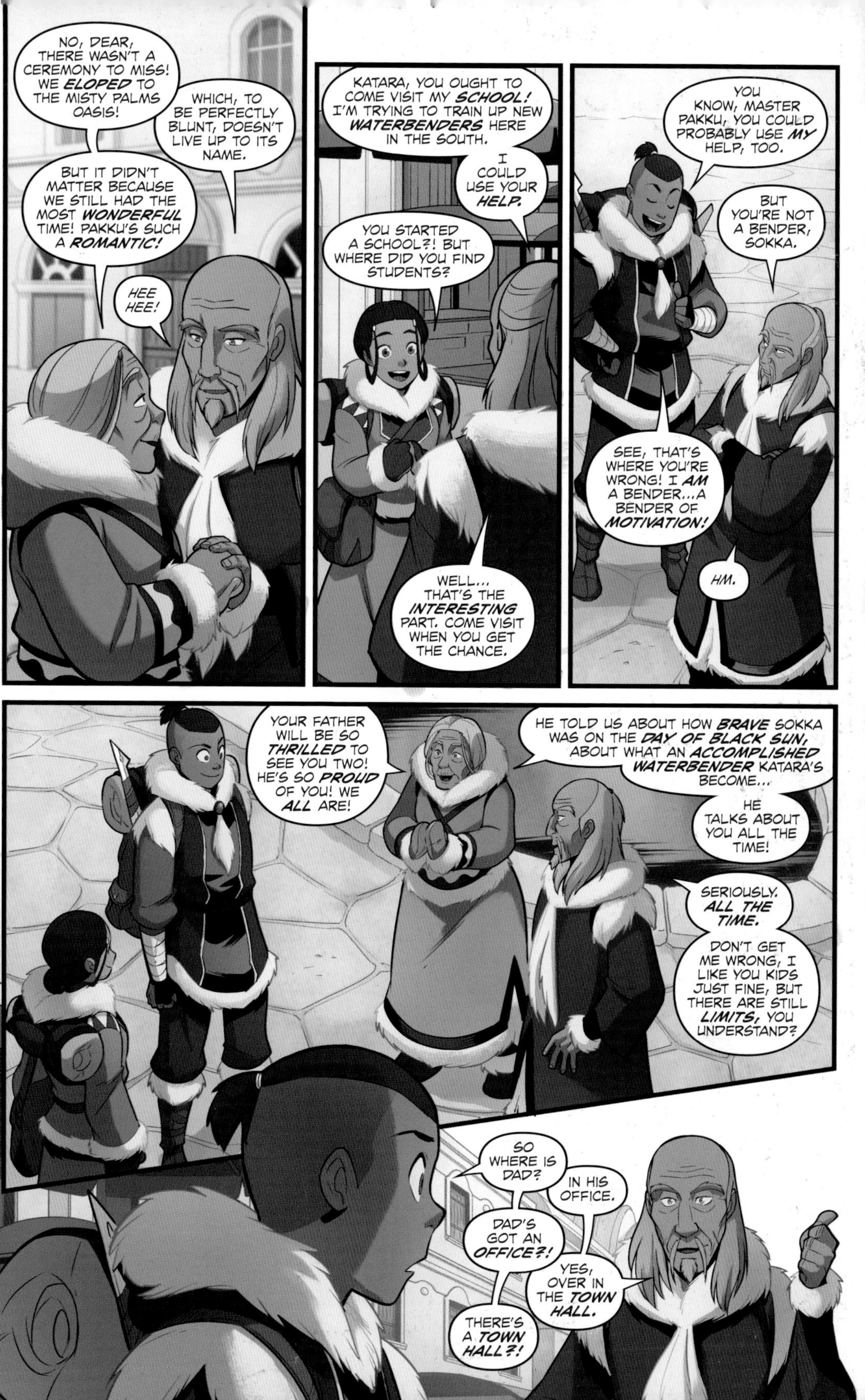
NO, DEAR, THERE WASN'T A CEREMONY TO MISS! WE ELOPED TO THE MISTY PALMS OASIS!
WHICH, TO BE PERFECTLY BLUNT, DOESN'T LIVE UP TO ITS NAME.
BUT IT DIDN'T MATTER BECAUSE WE STILL HAD THE MOST WONDERFUL TIME! PAKKU'S SUCH A ROMANTIC!
HEE HEE!
KATARA, YOU OUGHT TO COME VISIT MY SCHOOL! I'M TRYING TO TRAIN UP NEW WATERBENDERS HERE IN THE SOUTH.
I COULD USE YOUR HELP.
YOU STARTED A SCHOOL?! BUT WHERE DID YOU FIND STUDENTS?
WELL... THAT'S THE INTERESTING PART. COME VISIT WHEN YOU GET THE CHANCE.
YOU KNOW, MASTER PAKKU, YOU COULD PROBABLY USE MY HELP, TOO.
BUT YOU'RE NOT A BENDER, SOKKA.
SEE, THAT'S WHERE YOU'RE WRONG! I AM A BENDER...A BENDER OF MOTIVATION!
HM.
YOUR FATHER WILL BE SO THRILLED TO SEE YOU TWO! HE'S SO PROUD OF YOU! WE ALL ARE!
HE TOLD US ABOUT HOW BRAVE SOKKA WAS ON THE DAY OF BLACK SUN, ABOUT WHAT AN ACCOMPLISHED WATERBENDER KATARA'S BECOME...
HE TALKS ABOUT YOU ALL THE TIME!
SERIOUSLY. ALL THE TIME.
DON'T GET ME WRONG, I LIKE YOU KIDS JUST FINE, BUT THERE ARE STILL LIMITS, YOU UNDERSTAND?
SO WHERE IS DAD?
IN HIS OFFICE.
DAD'S GOT AN OFFICE?!
YES, OVER IN THE TOWN HALL.
THERE'S A TOWN HALL?!

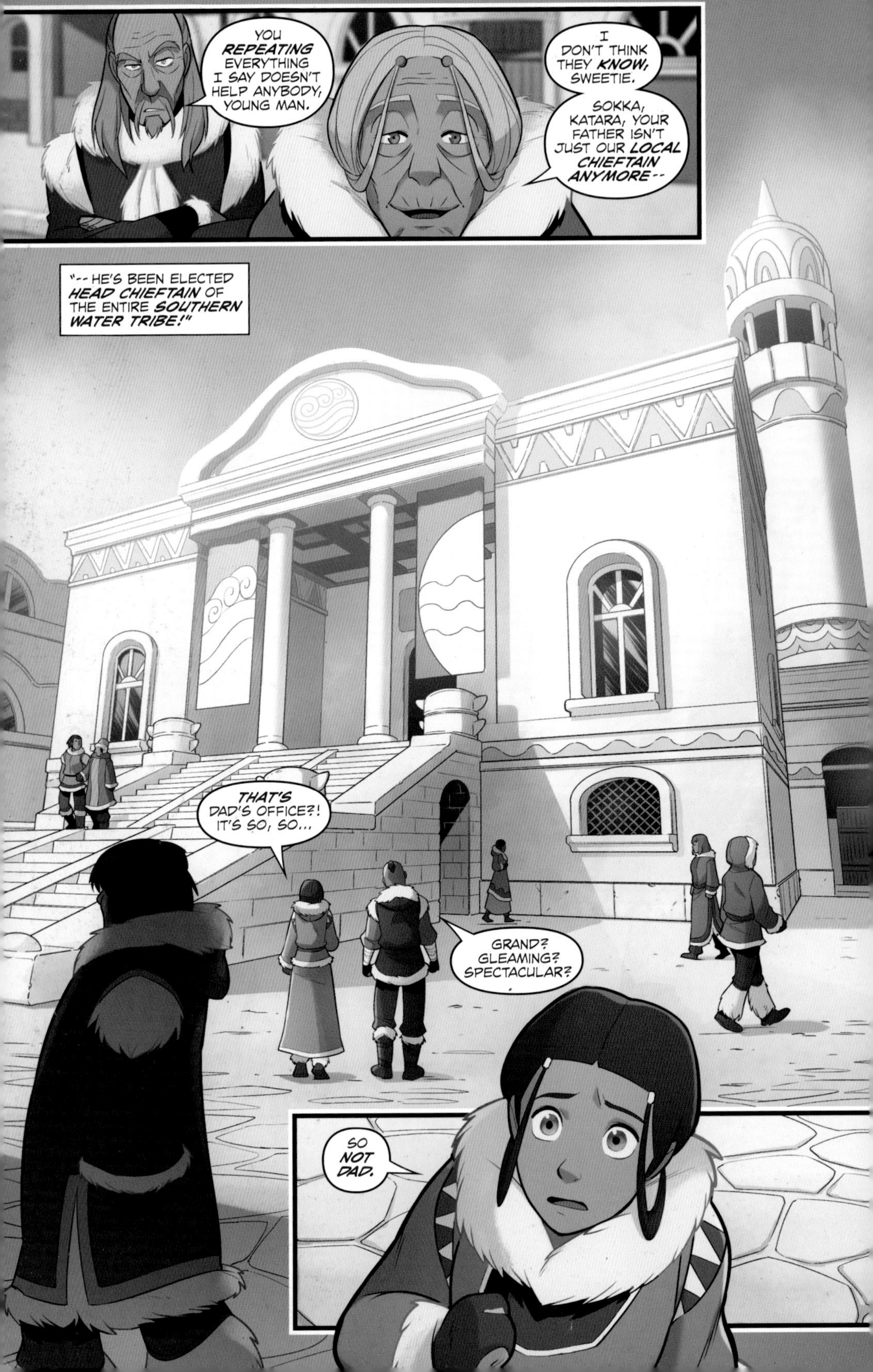
YOU *REPEATING* EVERYTHING I SAY DOESN'T HELP ANYBODY, YOUNG MAN.
I DON'T THINK THEY *KNOW,* SWEETIE.
SOKKA, KATARA, YOUR FATHER ISN'T JUST OUR *LOCAL CHIEFTAIN ANYMORE*--
"--HE'S BEEN ELECTED *HEAD CHIEFTAIN* OF THE ENTIRE *SOUTHERN WATER TRIBE!*"
THAT'S DAD'S OFFICE?! IT'S SO, SO...
GRAND? GLEAMING? SPECTACULAR?
SO *NOT DAD.*

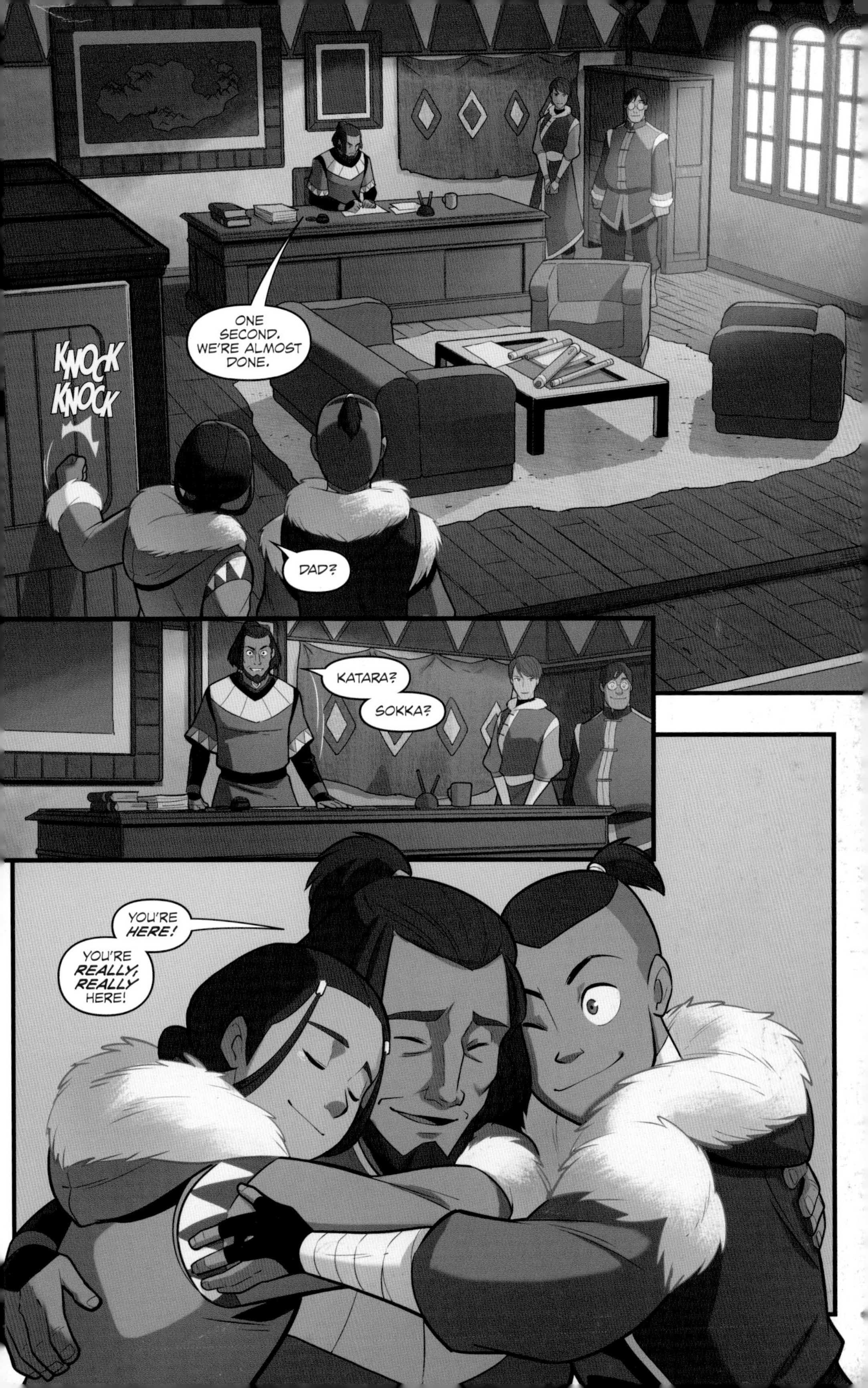
ONE SECOND. WE'RE ALMOST DONE.
KNOCK KNOCK
DAD?
KATARA?
SOKKA?
YOU'RE *HERE!*
YOU'RE *REALLY, REALLY* HERE!

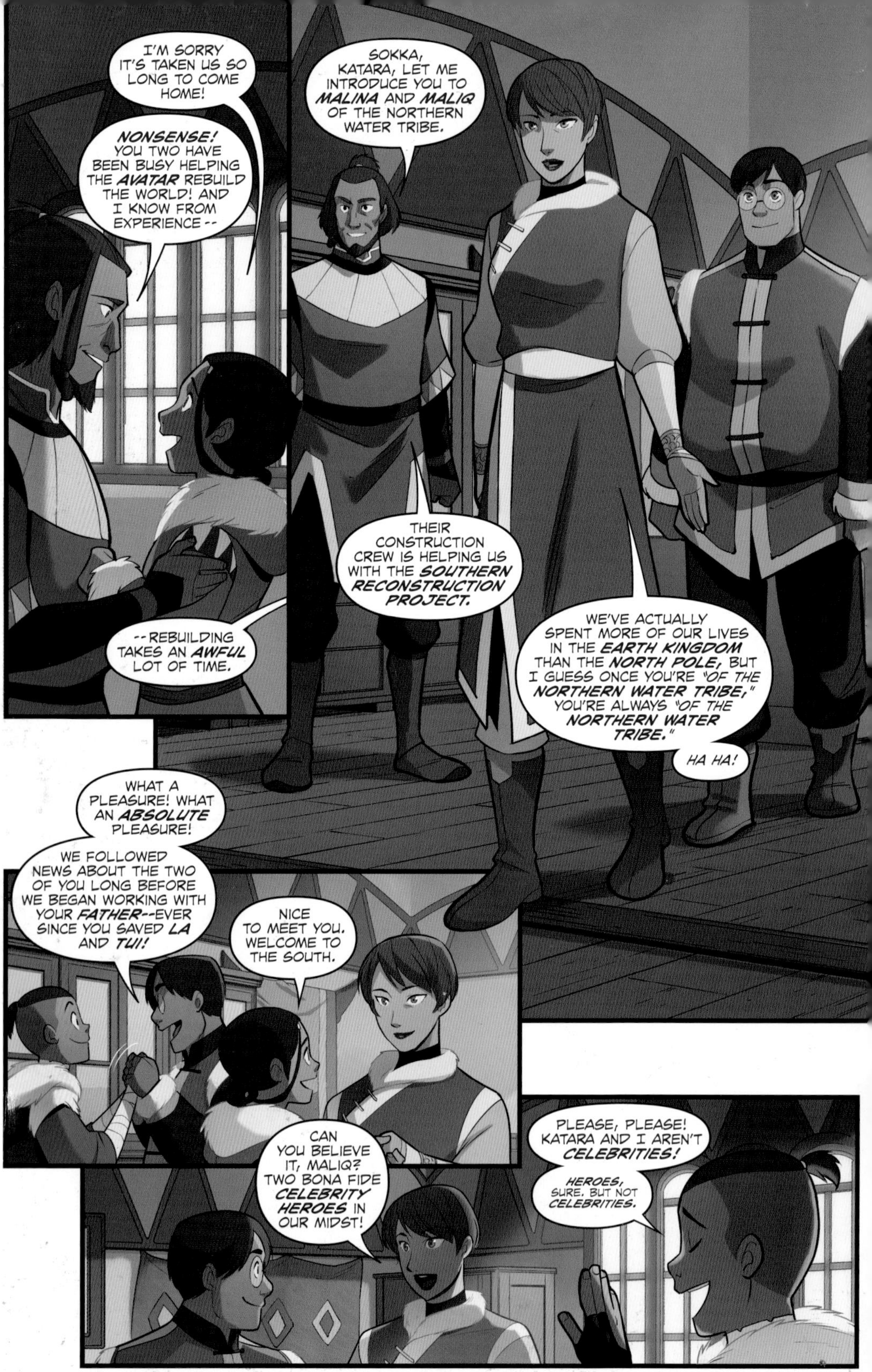
I'M SORRY IT'S TAKEN US SO LONG TO COME HOME!
NONSENSE! YOU TWO HAVE BEEN BUSY HELPING THE AVATAR REBUILD THE WORLD! AND I KNOW FROM EXPERIENCE --
-- REBUILDING TAKES AN AWFUL LOT OF TIME.
SOKKA, KATARA, LET ME INTRODUCE YOU TO MALINA AND MALIQ OF THE NORTHERN WATER TRIBE.
THEIR CONSTRUCTION CREW IS HELPING US WITH THE SOUTHERN RECONSTRUCTION PROJECT.
WE'VE ACTUALLY SPENT MORE OF OUR LIVES IN THE EARTH KINGDOM THAN THE NORTH POLE, BUT I GUESS ONCE YOU'RE "OF THE NORTHERN WATER TRIBE," YOU'RE ALWAYS "OF THE NORTHERN WATER TRIBE."
HA HA!
WHAT A PLEASURE! WHAT AN ABSOLUTE PLEASURE!
WE FOLLOWED NEWS ABOUT THE TWO OF YOU LONG BEFORE WE BEGAN WORKING WITH YOUR FATHER--EVER SINCE YOU SAVED LA AND TUI!
NICE TO MEET YOU. WELCOME TO THE SOUTH.
CAN YOU BELIEVE IT, MALIQ? TWO BONA FIDE CELEBRITY HEROES IN OUR MIDST!
PLEASE, PLEASE! KATARA AND I AREN'T CELEBRITIES!
HEROES, SURE. BUT NOT CELEBRITIES.

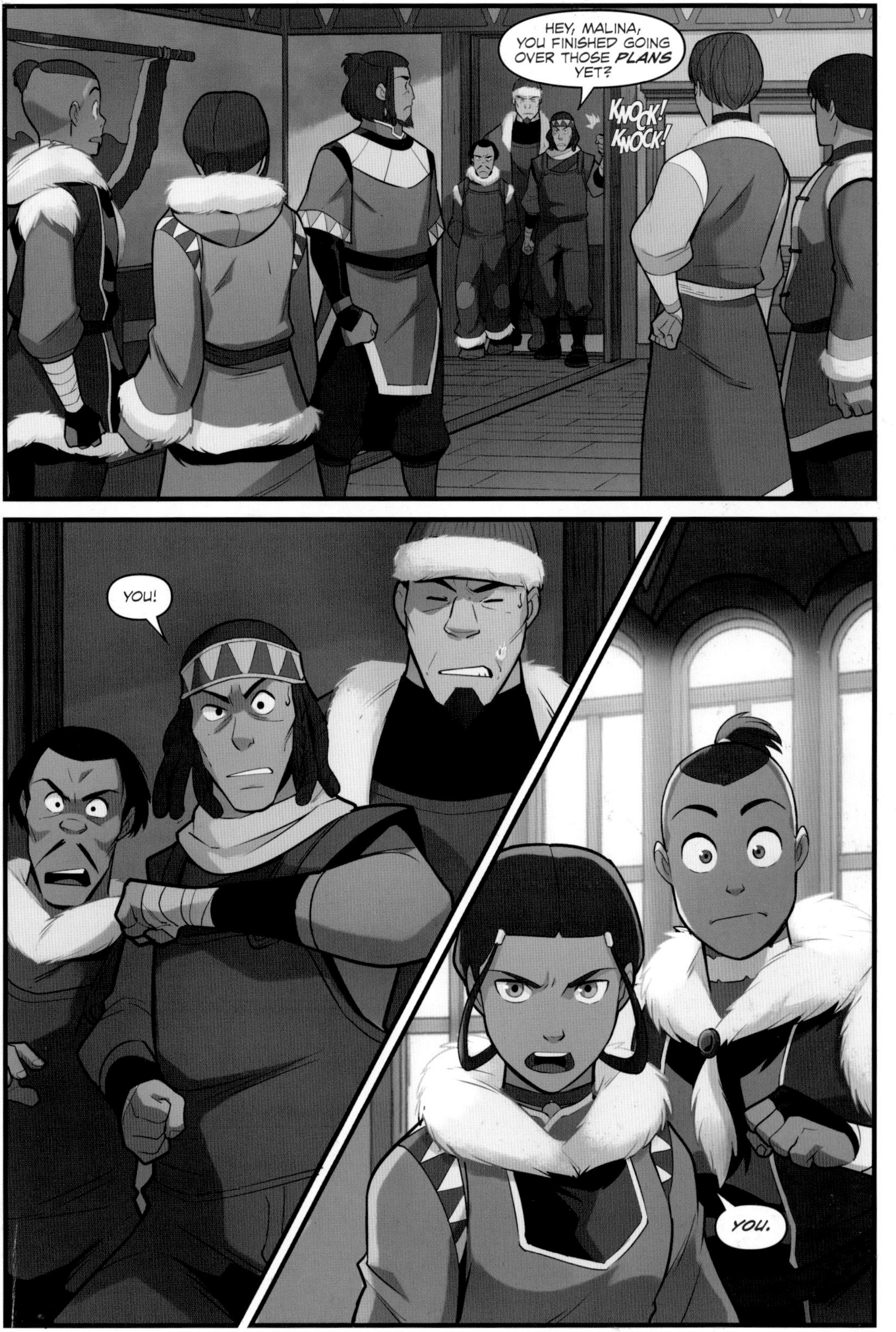
HEY, MALINA, YOU FINISHED GOING OVER THOSE PLANS YET?
KNOCK! KNOCK!
YOU!
YOU.

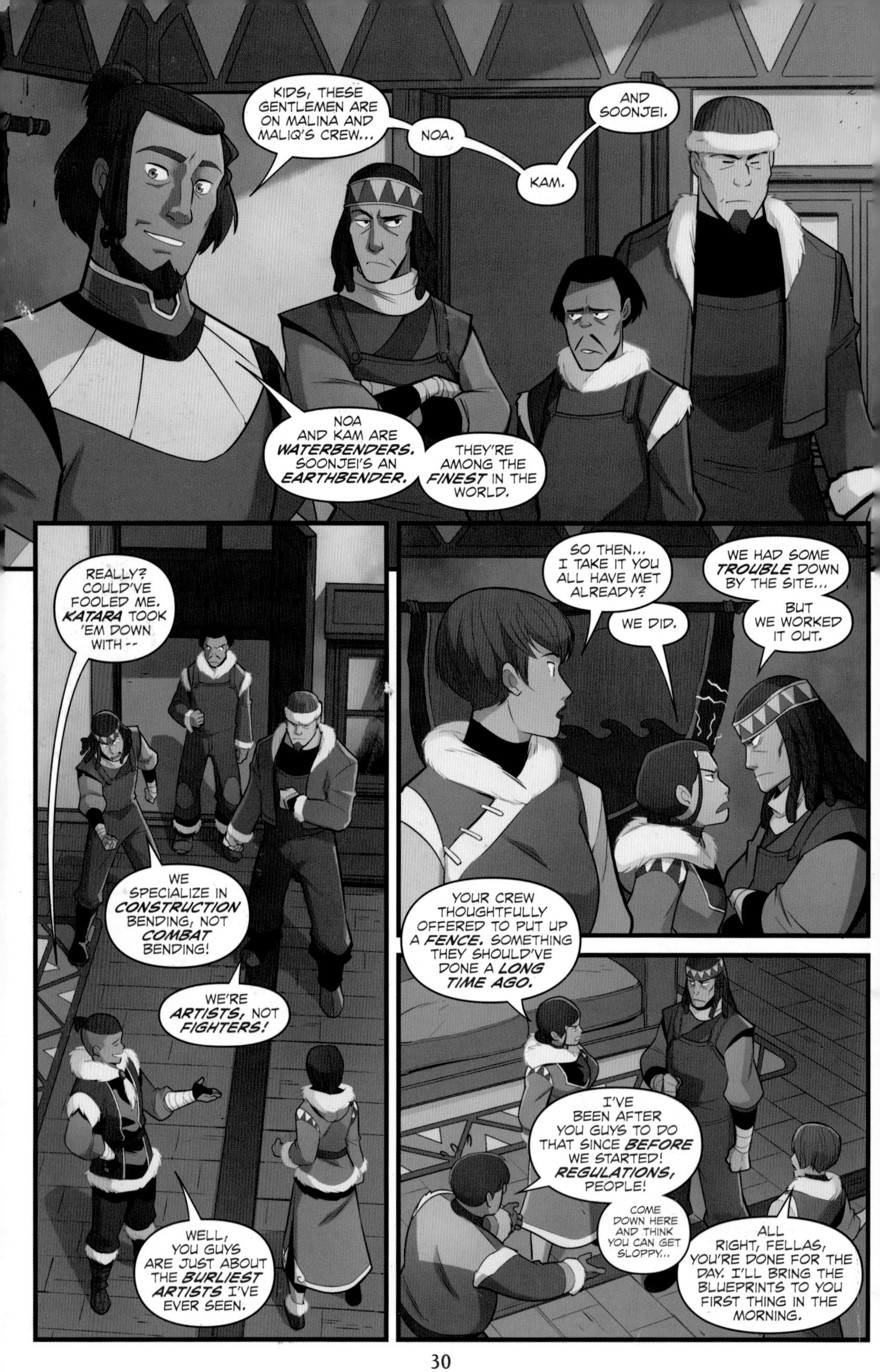
KIDS, THESE GENTLEMEN ARE ON MALINA AND MALIQ'S CREW...
NOA.
KAM.
AND SOONJEI.
NOA AND KAM ARE WATERBENDERS. SOONJEI'S AN EARTHBENDER.
THEY'RE AMONG THE FINEST IN THE WORLD.
REALLY? COULD'VE FOOLED ME. KATARA TOOK 'EM DOWN WITH --
WE SPECIALIZE IN CONSTRUCTION BENDING, NOT COMBAT BENDING!
WE'RE ARTISTS, NOT FIGHTERS!
WELL, YOU GUYS ARE JUST ABOUT THE BURLIEST ARTISTS I'VE EVER SEEN.
SO THEN... I TAKE IT YOU ALL HAVE MET ALREADY?
WE DID.
WE HAD SOME TROUBLE DOWN BY THE SITE...
BUT WE WORKED IT OUT.
YOUR CREW THOUGHTFULLY OFFERED TO PUT UP A FENCE. SOMETHING THEY SHOULD'VE DONE A LONG TIME AGO.
I'VE BEEN AFTER YOU GUYS TO DO THAT SINCE BEFORE WE STARTED! REGULATIONS, PEOPLE!
COME DOWN HERE AND THINK YOU CAN GET SLOPPY...
ALL RIGHT, FELLAS, YOU'RE DONE FOR THE DAY. I'LL BRING THE BLUEPRINTS TO YOU FIRST THING IN THE MORNING.

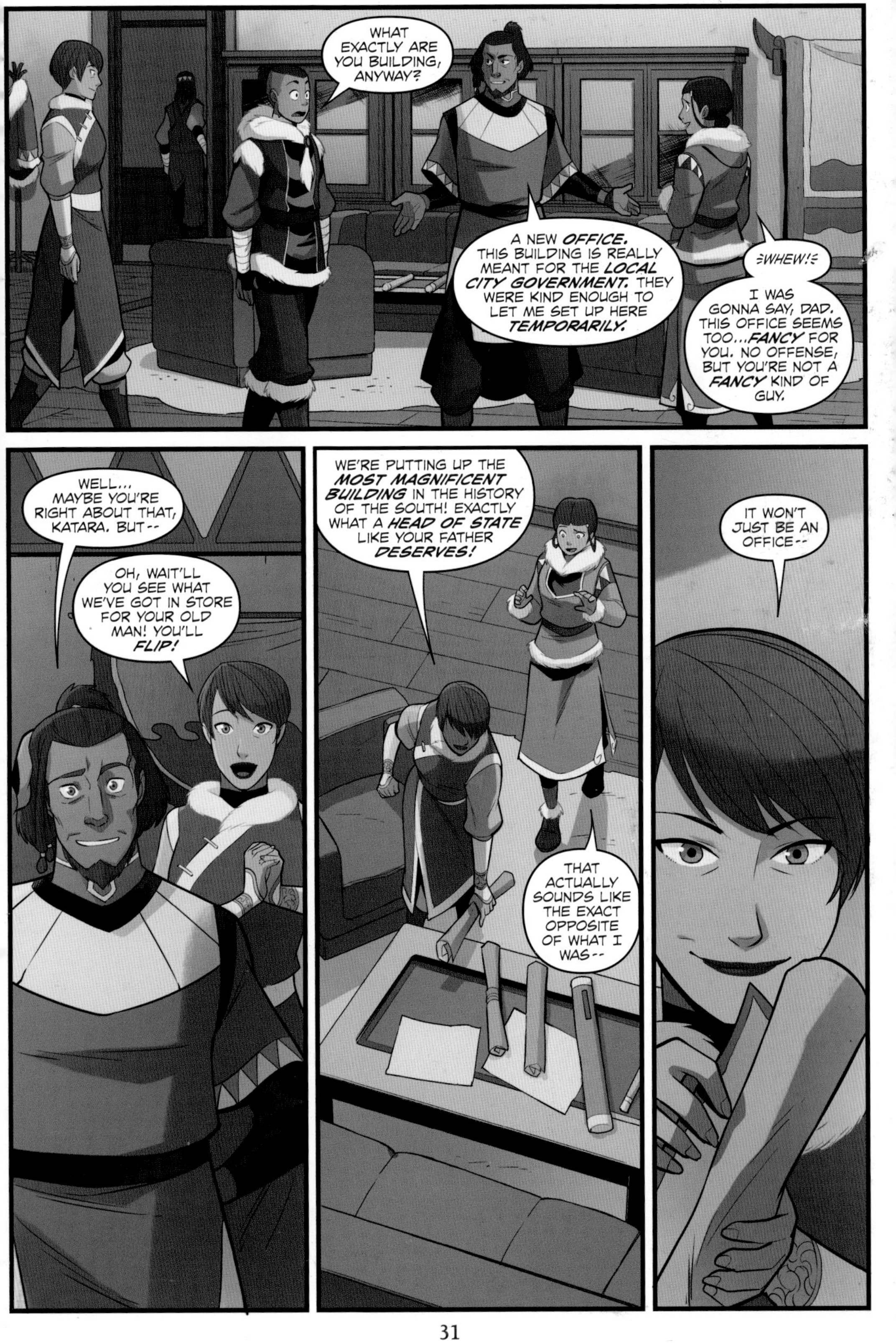
WHAT EXACTLY ARE YOU BUILDING, ANYWAY?
A NEW OFFICE. THIS BUILDING IS REALLY MEANT FOR THE LOCAL CITY GOVERNMENT. THEY WERE KIND ENOUGH TO LET ME SET UP HERE TEMPORARILY.
WHEW!
I WAS GONNA SAY, DAD. THIS OFFICE SEEMS TOO...FANCY FOR YOU. NO OFFENSE, BUT YOU'RE NOT A FANCY KIND OF GUY.
WELL... MAYBE YOU'RE RIGHT ABOUT THAT, KATARA. BUT--
OH, WAIT'LL YOU SEE WHAT WE'VE GOT IN STORE FOR YOUR OLD MAN! YOU'LL FLIP!
WE'RE PUTTING UP THE MOST MAGNIFICENT BUILDING IN THE HISTORY OF THE SOUTH! EXACTLY WHAT A HEAD OF STATE LIKE YOUR FATHER DESERVES!
THAT ACTUALLY SOUNDS LIKE THE EXACT OPPOSITE OF WHAT I WAS--
IT WON'T JUST BE AN OFFICE--

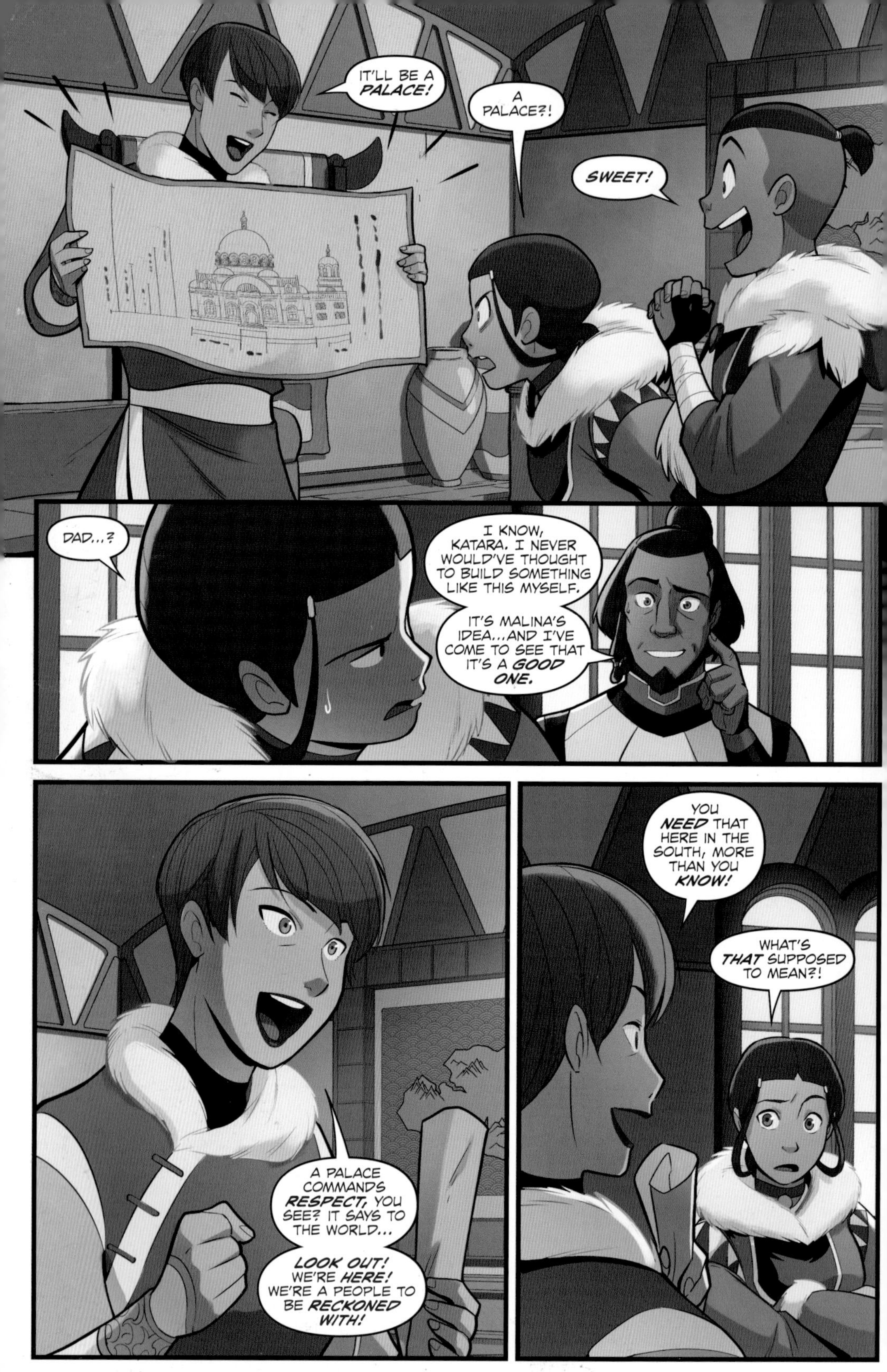
IT'LL BE A PALACE!
A PALACE?!
SWEET!
DAD...?
I KNOW, KATARA. I NEVER WOULD'VE THOUGHT TO BUILD SOMETHING LIKE THIS MYSELF.
IT'S MALINA'S IDEA...AND I'VE COME TO SEE THAT IT'S A GOOD ONE.
A PALACE COMMANDS RESPECT, YOU SEE? IT SAYS TO THE WORLD...
LOOK OUT! WE'RE HERE! WE'RE A PEOPLE TO BE RECKONED WITH!
YOU NEED THAT HERE IN THE SOUTH, MORE THAN YOU KNOW!
WHAT'S THAT SUPPOSED TO MEAN?!

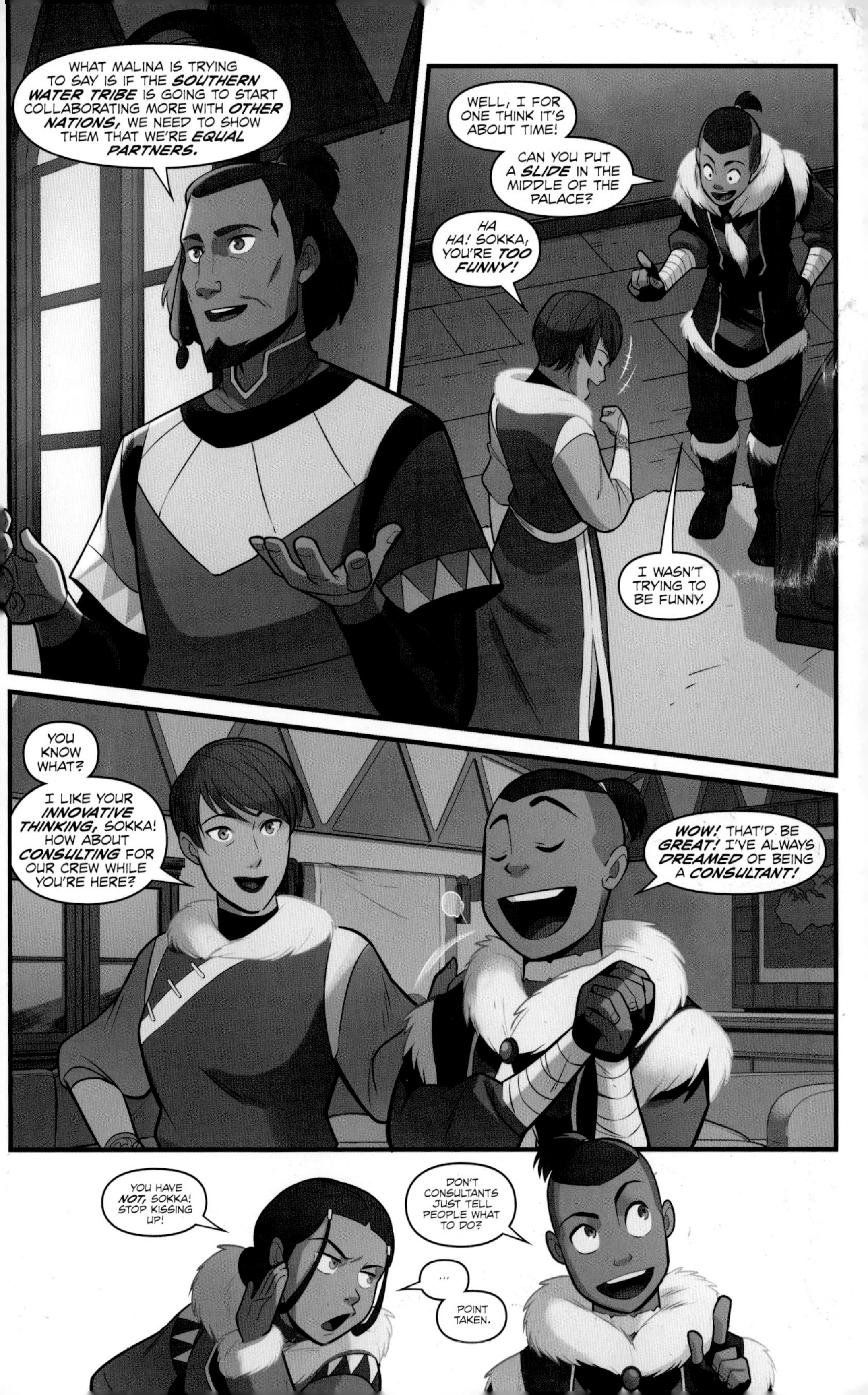
WHAT MALINA IS TRYING TO SAY IS IF THE SOUTHERN WATER TRIBE IS GOING TO START COLLABORATING MORE WITH OTHER NATIONS, WE NEED TO SHOW THEM THAT WE'RE EQUAL PARTNERS.
WELL, I FOR ONE THINK IT'S ABOUT TIME!
CAN YOU PUT A SLIDE IN THE MIDDLE OF THE PALACE?
HA HA! SOKKA, YOU'RE TOO FUNNY!
I WASN'T TRYING TO BE FUNNY.
YOU KNOW WHAT?
I LIKE YOUR INNOVATIVE THINKING, SOKKA! HOW ABOUT CONSULTING FOR OUR CREW WHILE YOU'RE HERE?
WOW! THAT'D BE GREAT! I'VE ALWAYS DREAMED OF BEING A CONSULTANT!
YOU HAVE NOT, SOKKA! STOP KISSING UP!
DON'T CONSULTANTS JUST TELL PEOPLE WHAT TO DO?
...
POINT TAKEN.

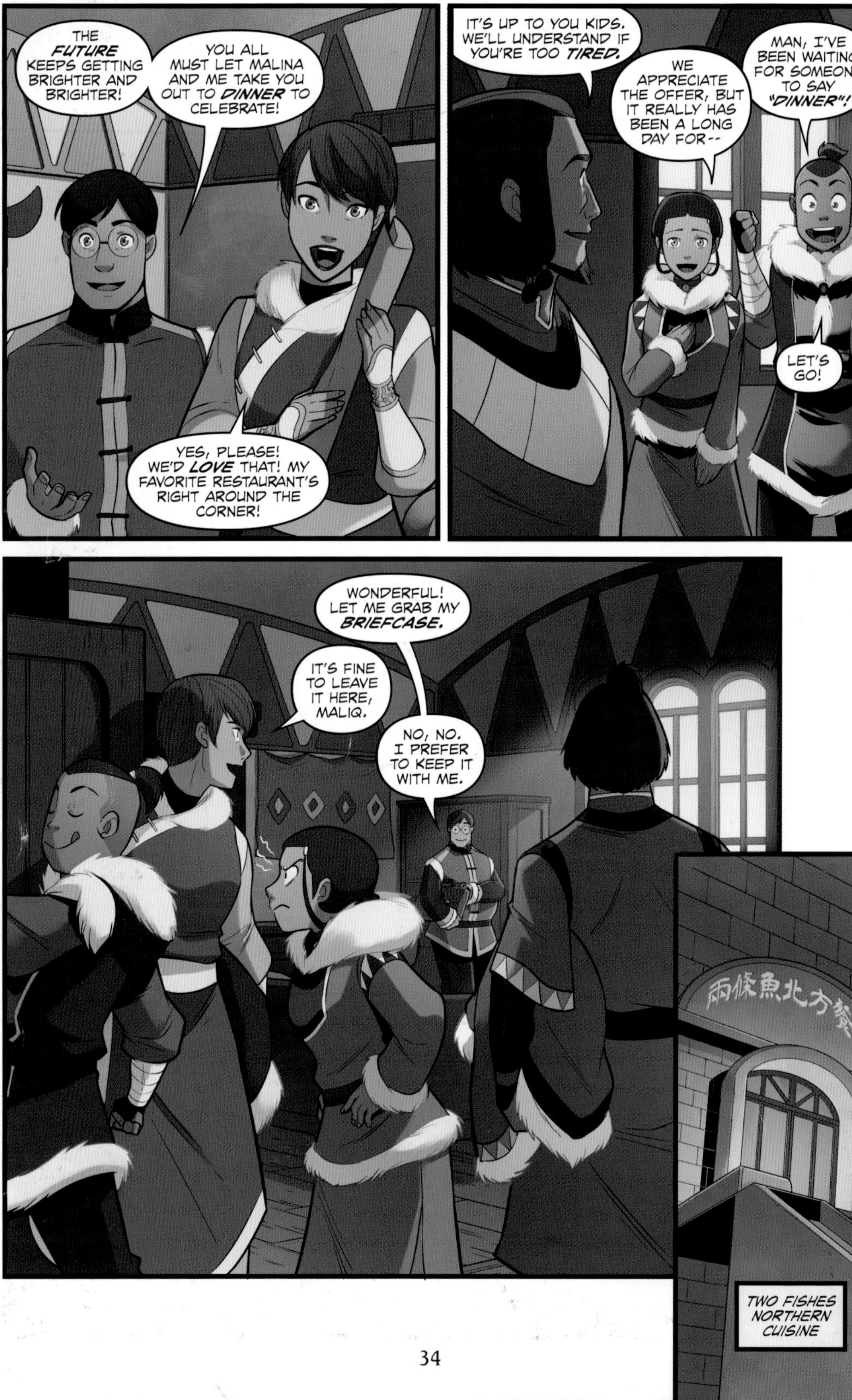
THE FUTURE KEEPS GETTING BRIGHTER AND BRIGHTER!
YOU ALL MUST LET MALINA AND ME TAKE YOU OUT TO DINNER TO CELEBRATE!
YES, PLEASE! WE'D LOVE THAT! MY FAVORITE RESTAURANT'S RIGHT AROUND THE CORNER!
IT'S UP TO YOU KIDS. WE'LL UNDERSTAND IF YOU'RE TOO TIRED.
WE APPRECIATE THE OFFER, BUT IT REALLY HAS BEEN A LONG DAY FOR--
MAN, I'VE BEEN WAITING FOR SOMEONE TO SAY "DINNER"!
LET'S GO!
WONDERFUL! LET ME GRAB MY BRIEFCASE.
IT'S FINE TO LEAVE IT HERE, MALIQ.
NO, NO. I PREFER TO KEEP IT WITH ME.
兩條魚北方餐館
TWO FISHES NORTHERN CUISINE

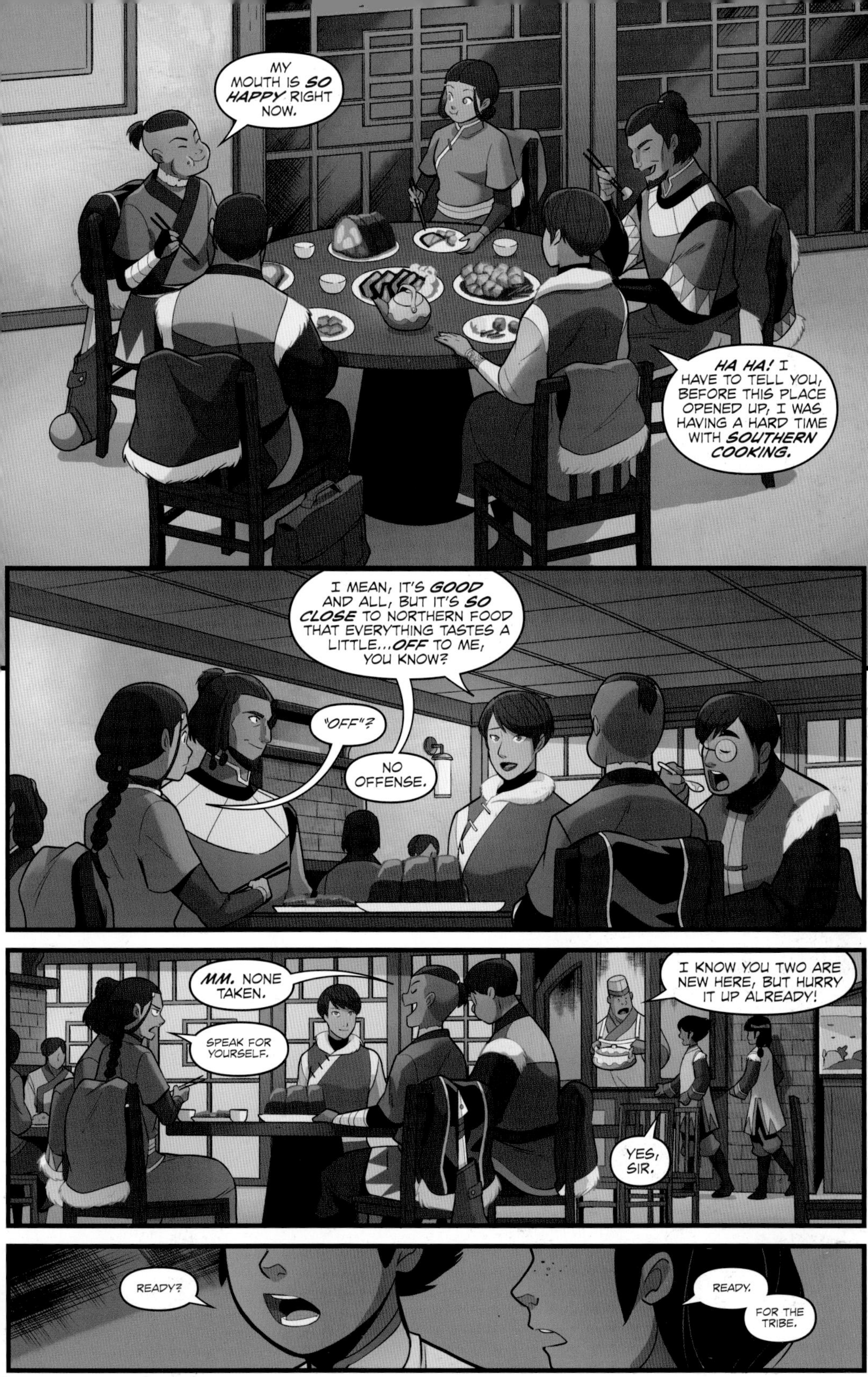
MY MOUTH IS SO HAPPY RIGHT NOW.
HA HA! I HAVE TO TELL YOU, BEFORE THIS PLACE OPENED UP, I WAS HAVING A HARD TIME WITH SOUTHERN COOKING.
I MEAN, IT'S GOOD AND ALL, BUT IT'S SO CLOSE TO NORTHERN FOOD THAT EVERYTHING TASTES A LITTLE...OFF TO ME, YOU KNOW?
"OFF"?
NO OFFENSE.
MM. NONE TAKEN.
SPEAK FOR YOURSELF.
I KNOW YOU TWO ARE NEW HERE, BUT HURRY IT UP ALREADY!
YES, SIR.
READY?
READY.
FOR THE TRIBE.

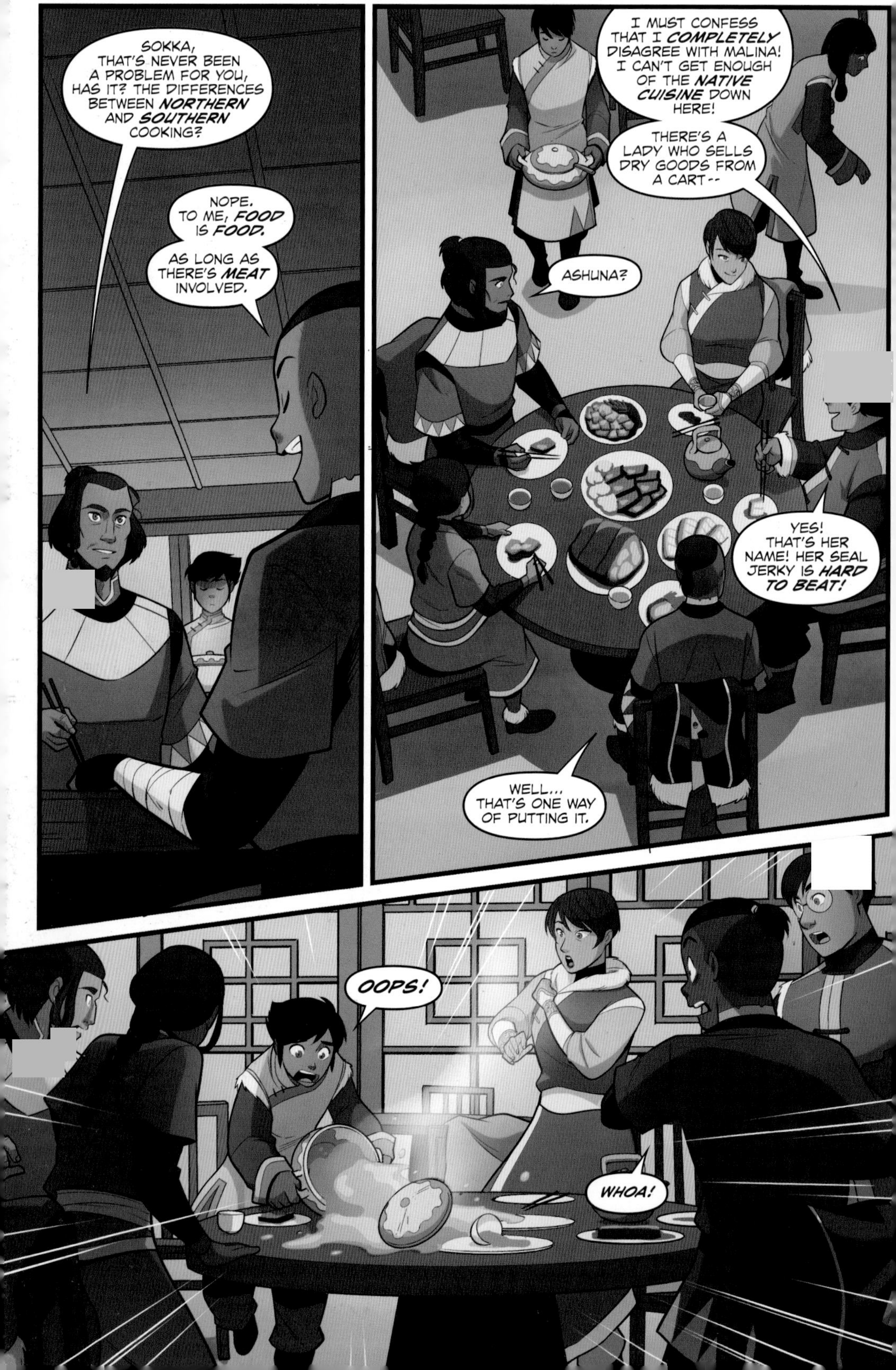
SOKKA, THAT'S NEVER BEEN A PROBLEM FOR YOU, HAS IT? THE DIFFERENCES BETWEEN NORTHERN AND SOUTHERN COOKING?
NOPE. TO ME, FOOD IS FOOD.
AS LONG AS THERE'S MEAT INVOLVED.
I MUST CONFESS THAT I COMPLETELY DISAGREE WITH MALINA! I CAN'T GET ENOUGH OF THE NATIVE CUISINE DOWN HERE!
THERE'S A LADY WHO SELLS DRY GOODS FROM A CART--
ASHUNA?
YES! THAT'S HER NAME! HER SEAL JERKY IS HARD TO BEAT!
WELL... THAT'S ONE WAY OF PUTTING IT.
OOPS!
WHOA!

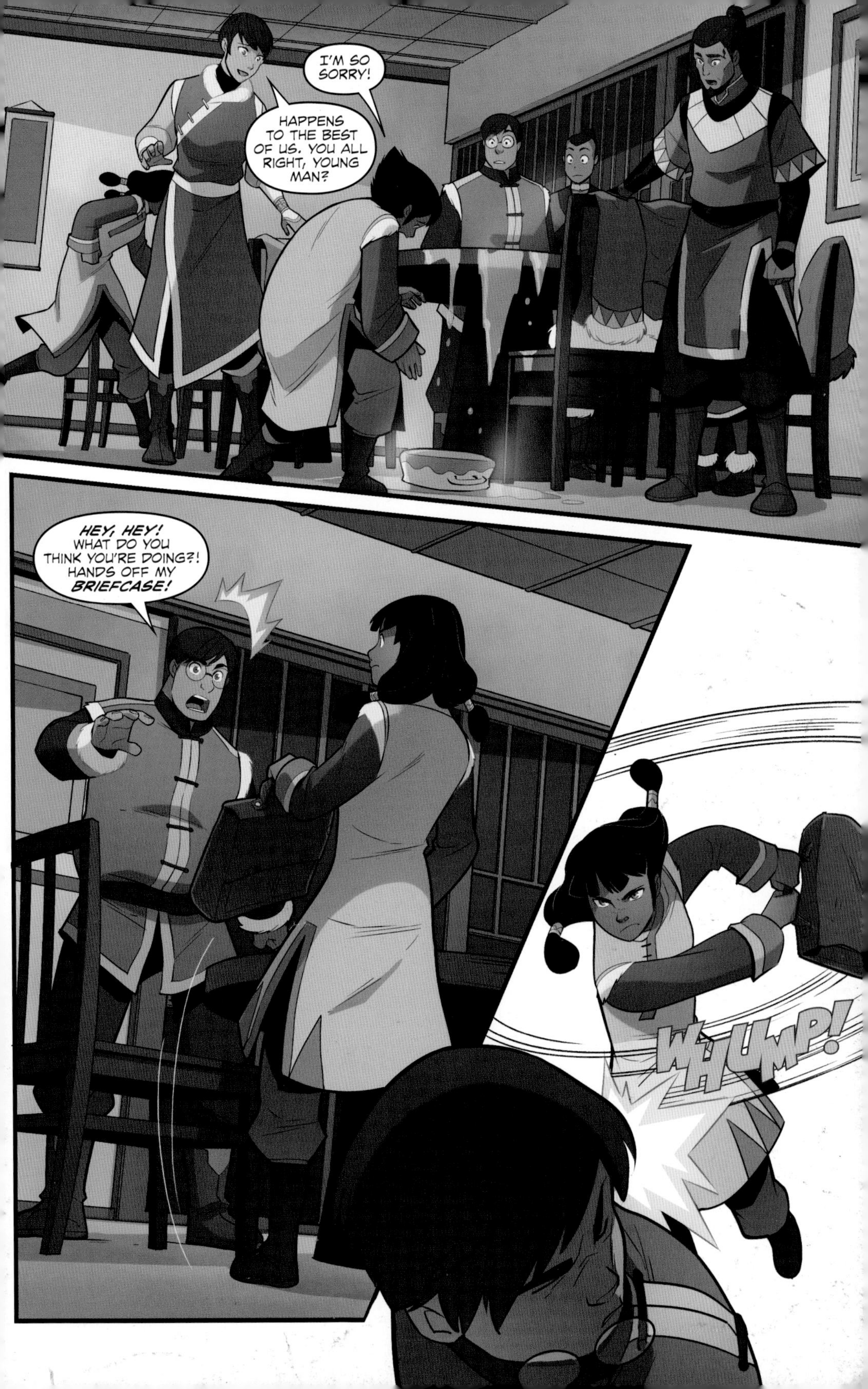
I'M SO SORRY!
HAPPENS TO THE BEST OF US. YOU ALL RIGHT, YOUNG MAN?
HEY, HEY! WHAT DO YOU THINK YOU'RE DOING?! HANDS OFF MY BRIEFCASE!
WHUMP!

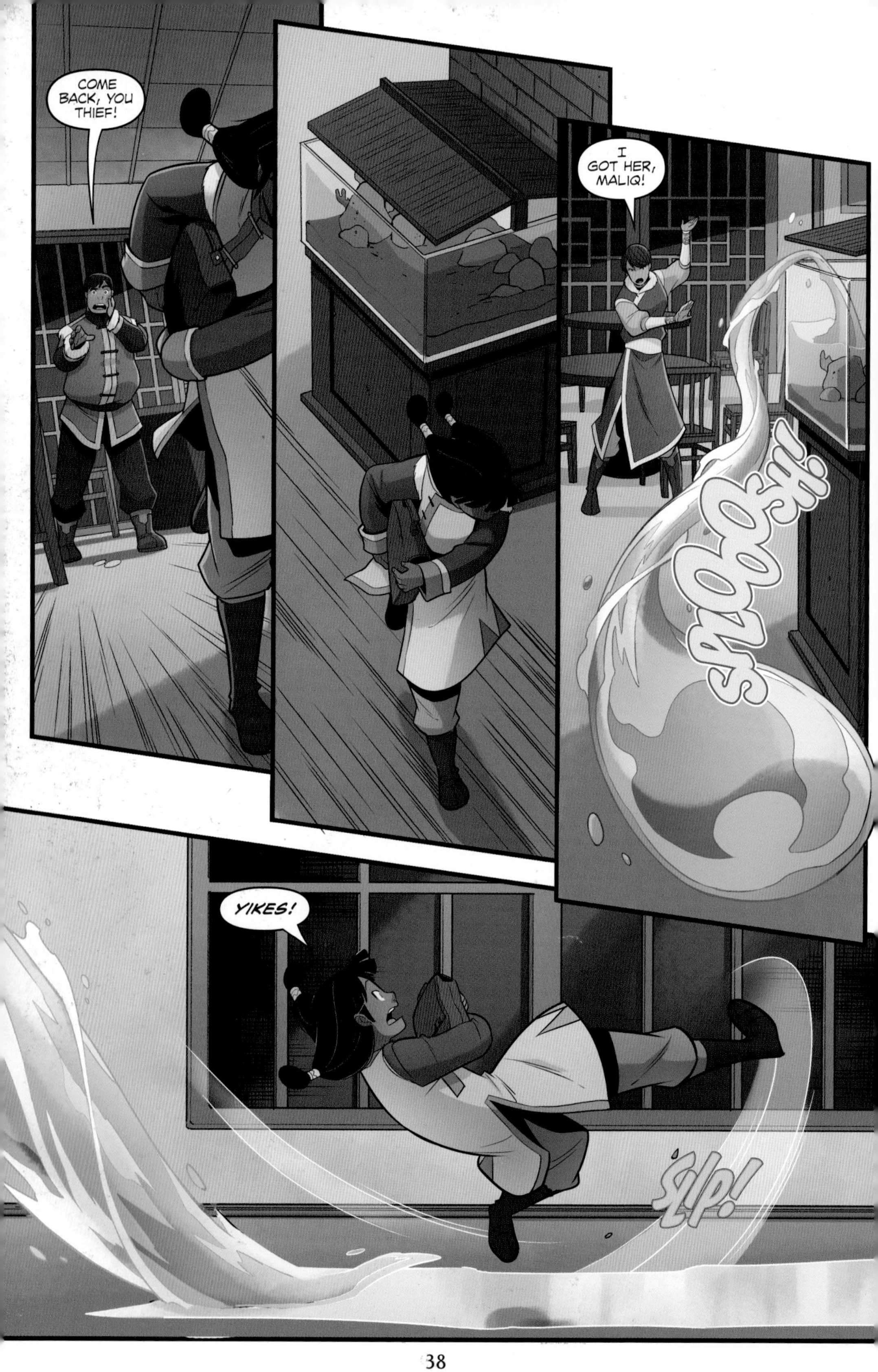
COME BACK, YOU THIEF!
I GOT HER, MALIQ!
SPLOOSH!
YIKES!
SLIP!

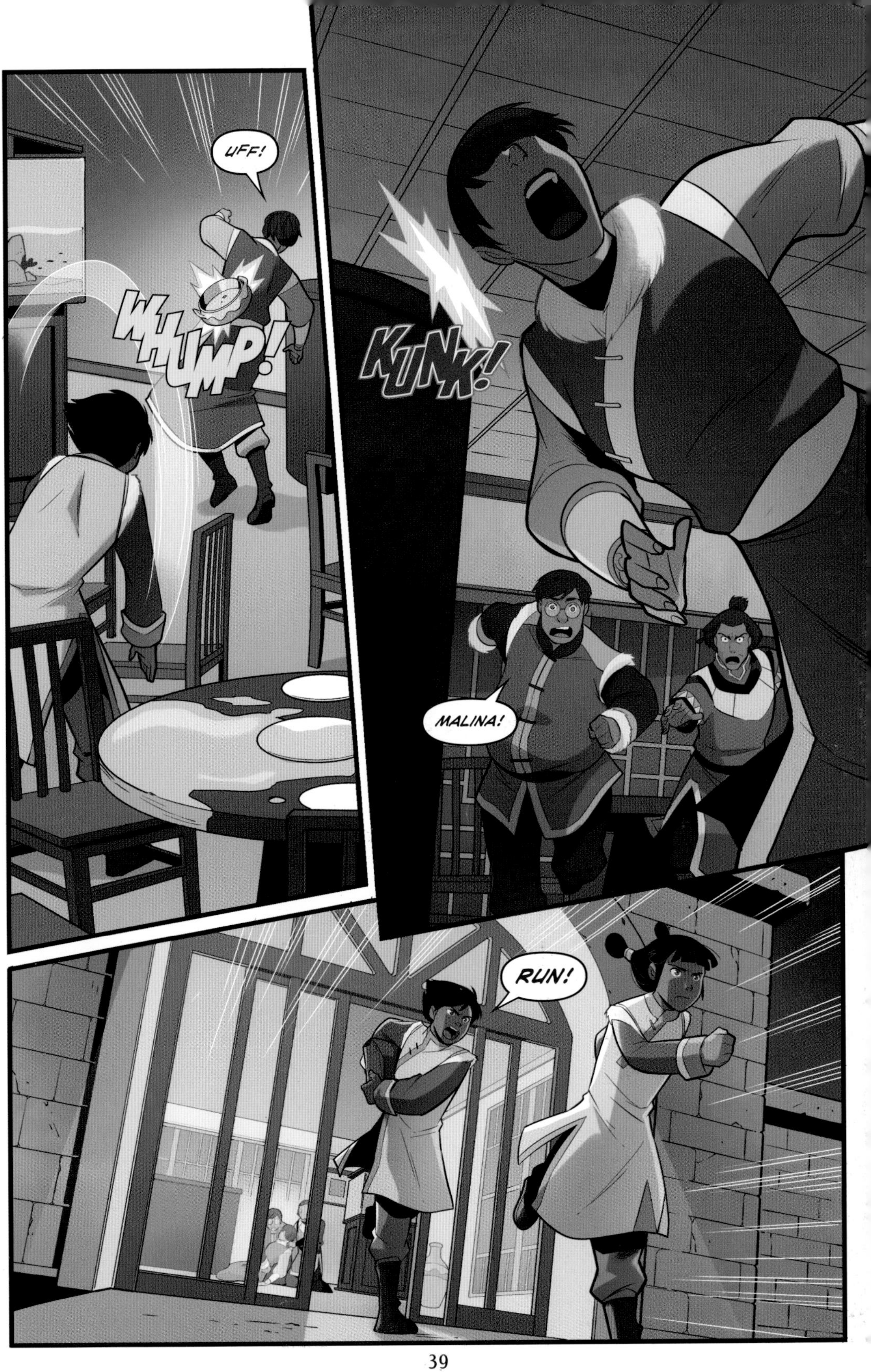
UFF!
WHUMP!
KUNK!
MALINA!
RUN!

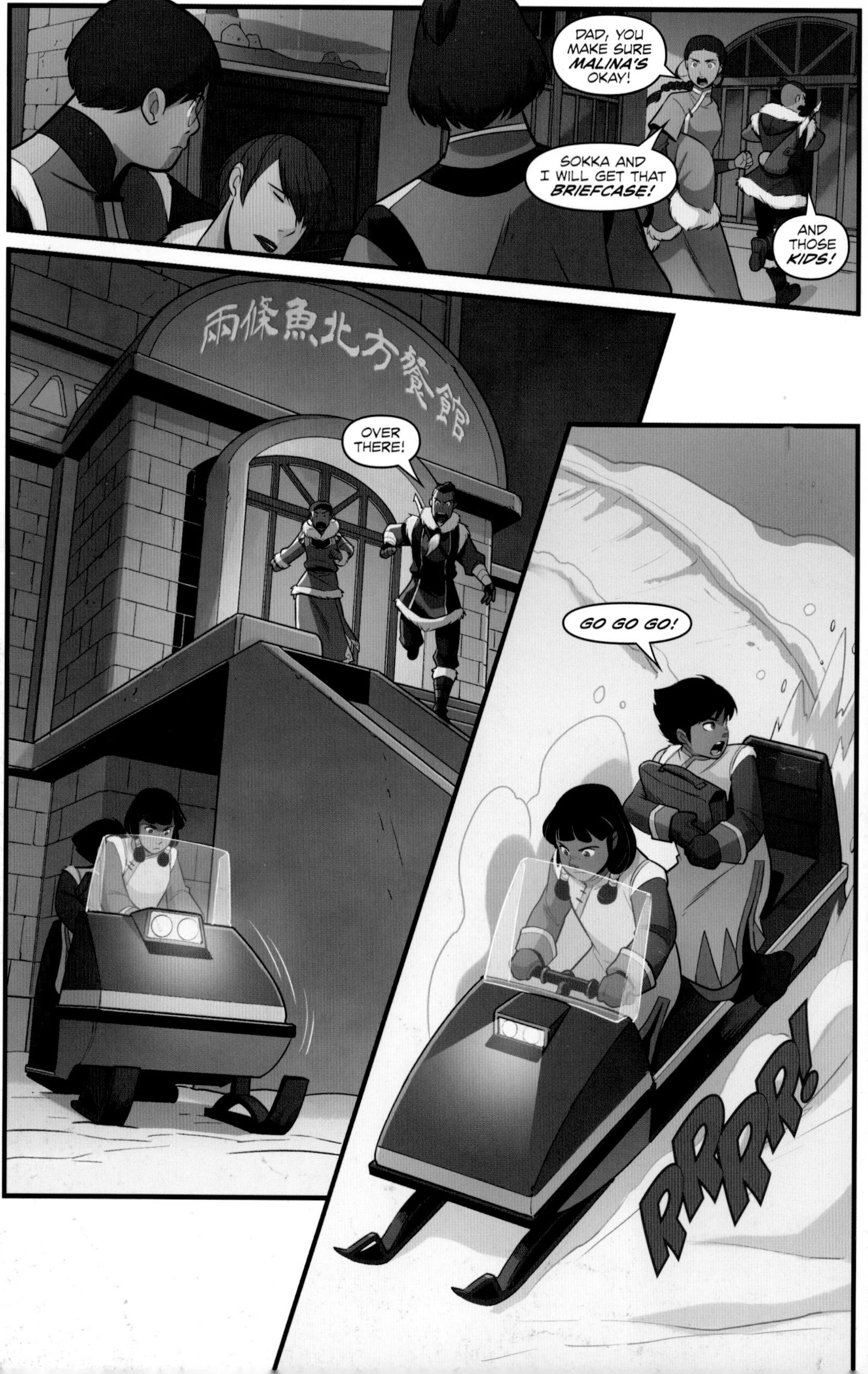
DAD, YOU MAKE SURE MALINA'S OKAY!
SOKKA AND I WILL GET THAT BRIEFCASE!
AND THOSE KIDS!
雨條魚北方餐館
OVER THERE!
GO GO GO!
RRRR!

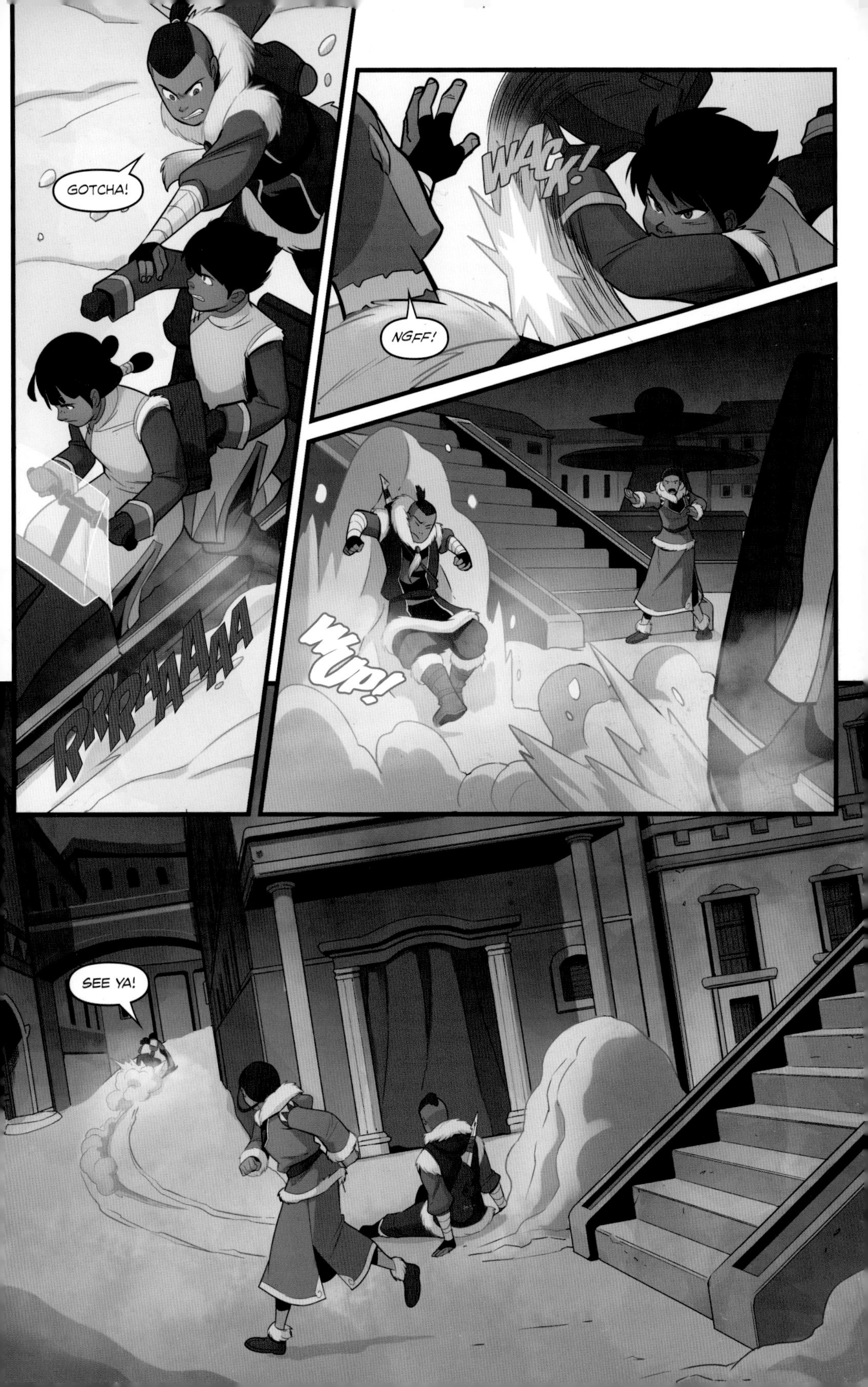
GOTCHA!
RRRAAAAAA
WACK!
NGFF!
WUP!
SEE YA!

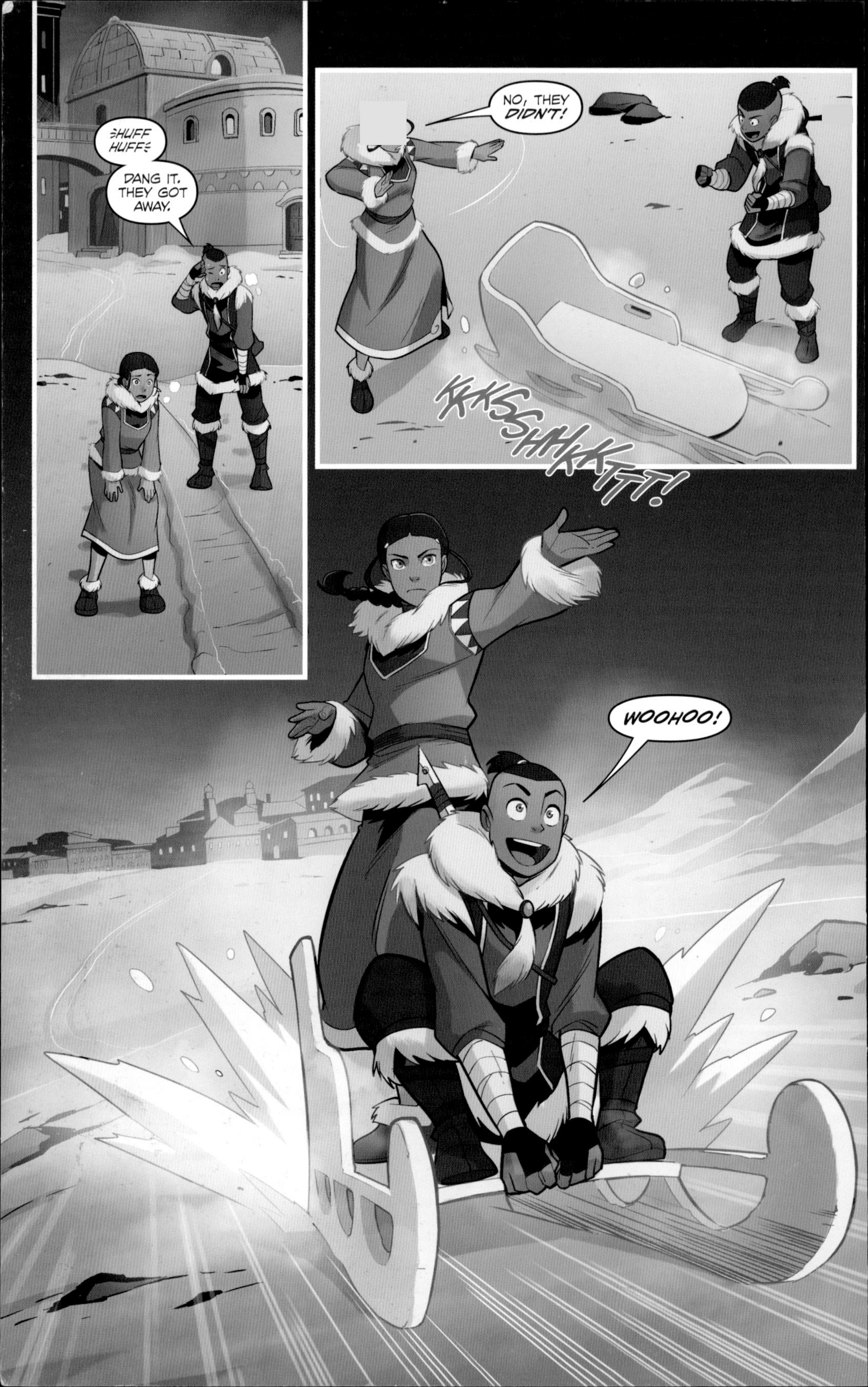

HUFF HUFF
DANG IT. THEY GOT AWAY.
NO, THEY DIDN'T!
KKKSSHHKKTTT!
WOOHOO!

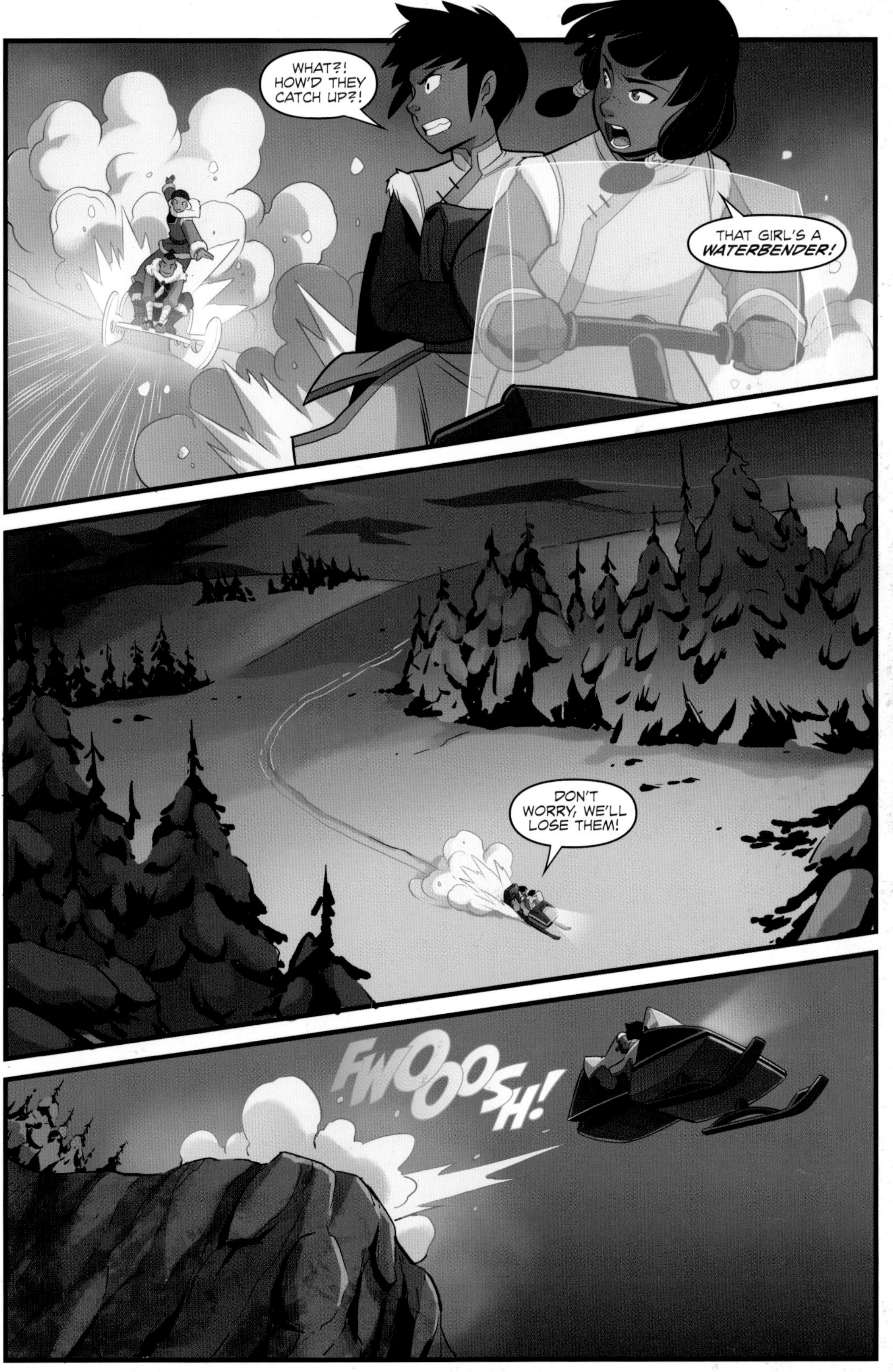
WHAT?! HOW'D THEY CATCH UP?!
THAT GIRL'S A WATERBENDER!
DON'T WORRY, WE'LL LOSE THEM!
FWOOOSH!

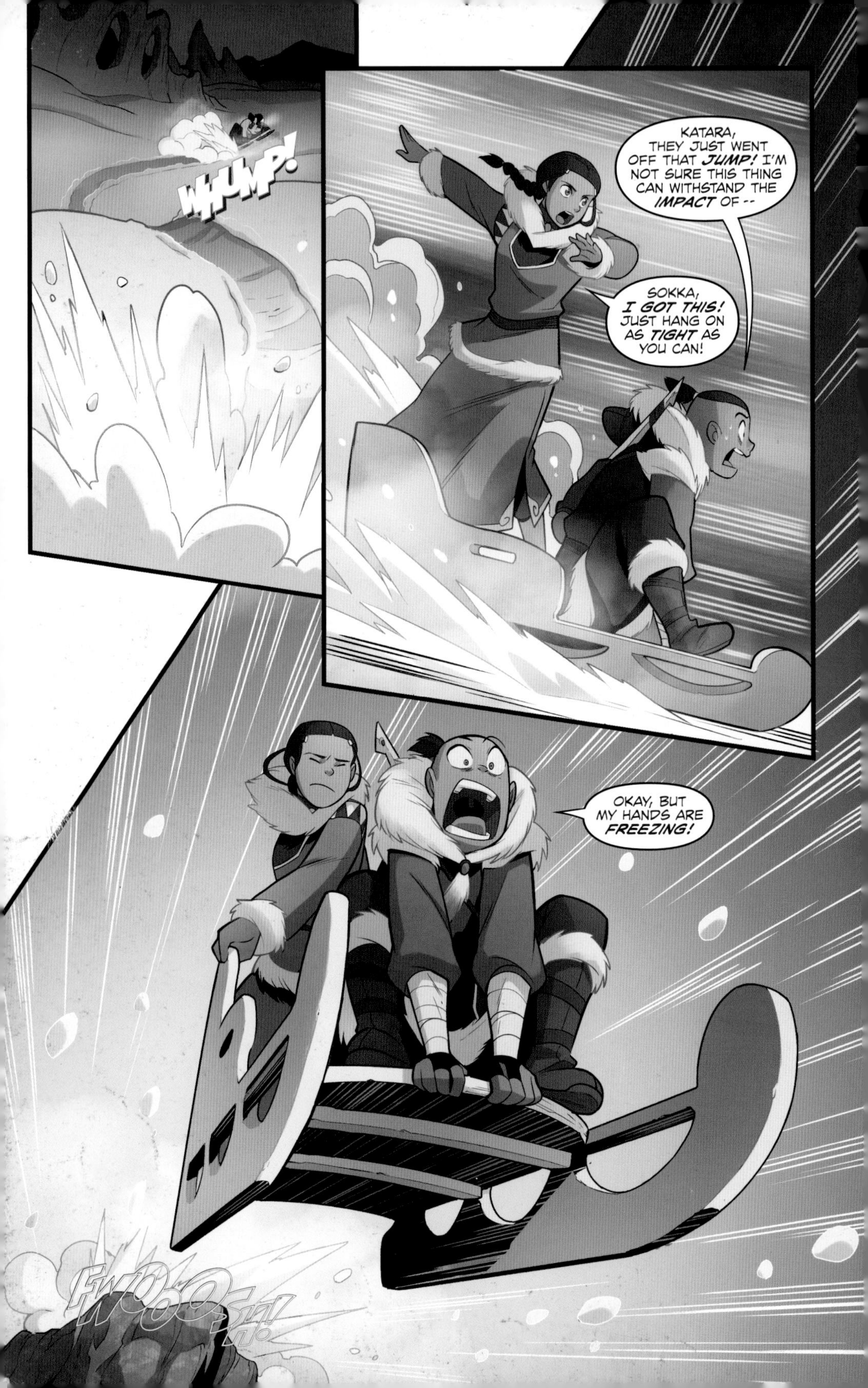
WHUMP!
KATARA, THEY JUST WENT OFF THAT JUMP! I'M NOT SURE THIS THING CAN WITHSTAND THE IMPACT OF --
SOKKA, I GOT THIS! JUST HANG ON AS TIGHT AS YOU CAN!
OKAY, BUT MY HANDS ARE FREEZING!
FWOOOOSH!

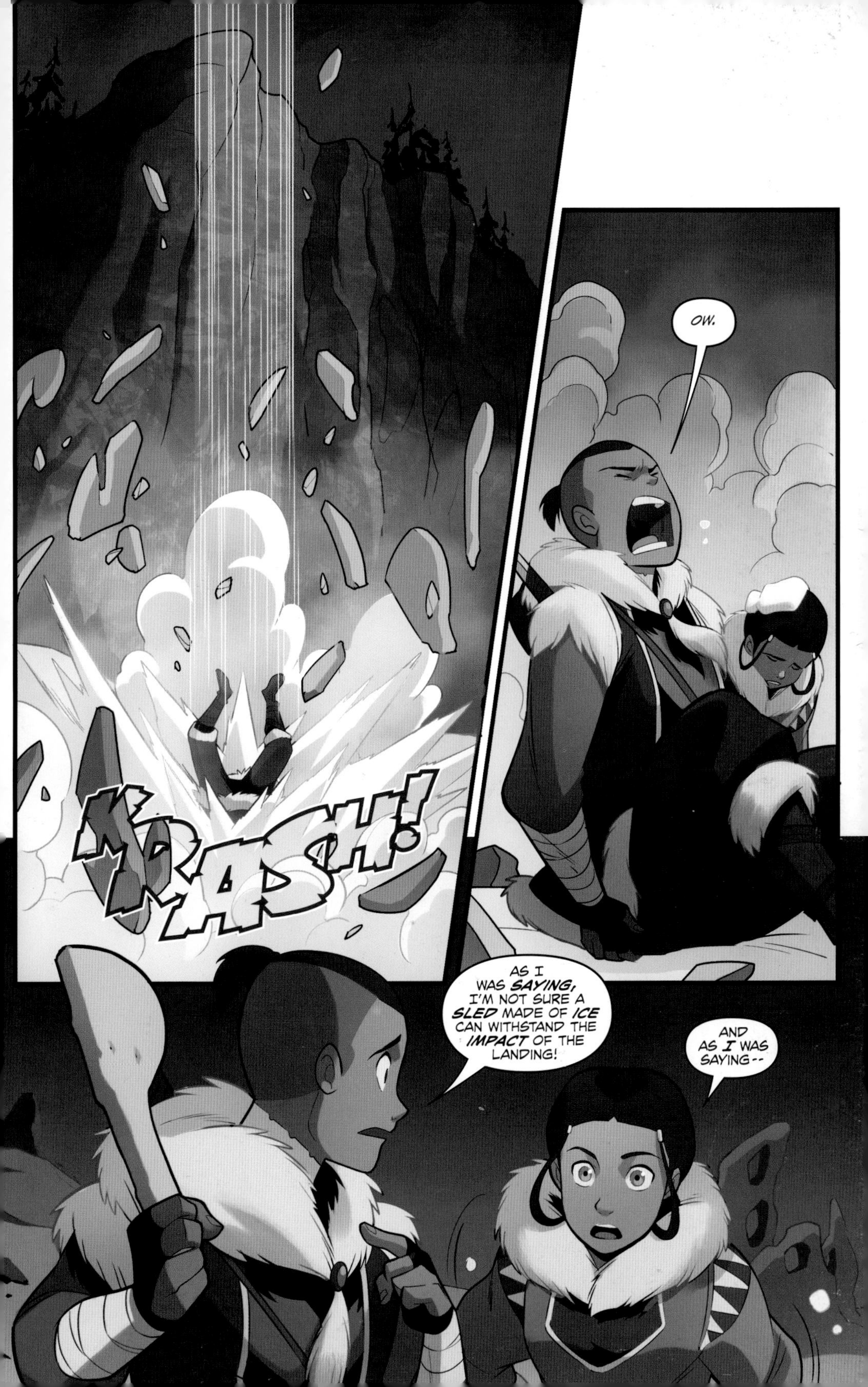
KRASH!
OW.
AS I WAS SAYING, I'M NOT SURE A SLED MADE OF ICE CAN WITHSTAND THE IMPACT OF THE LANDING!
AND AS I WAS SAYING--

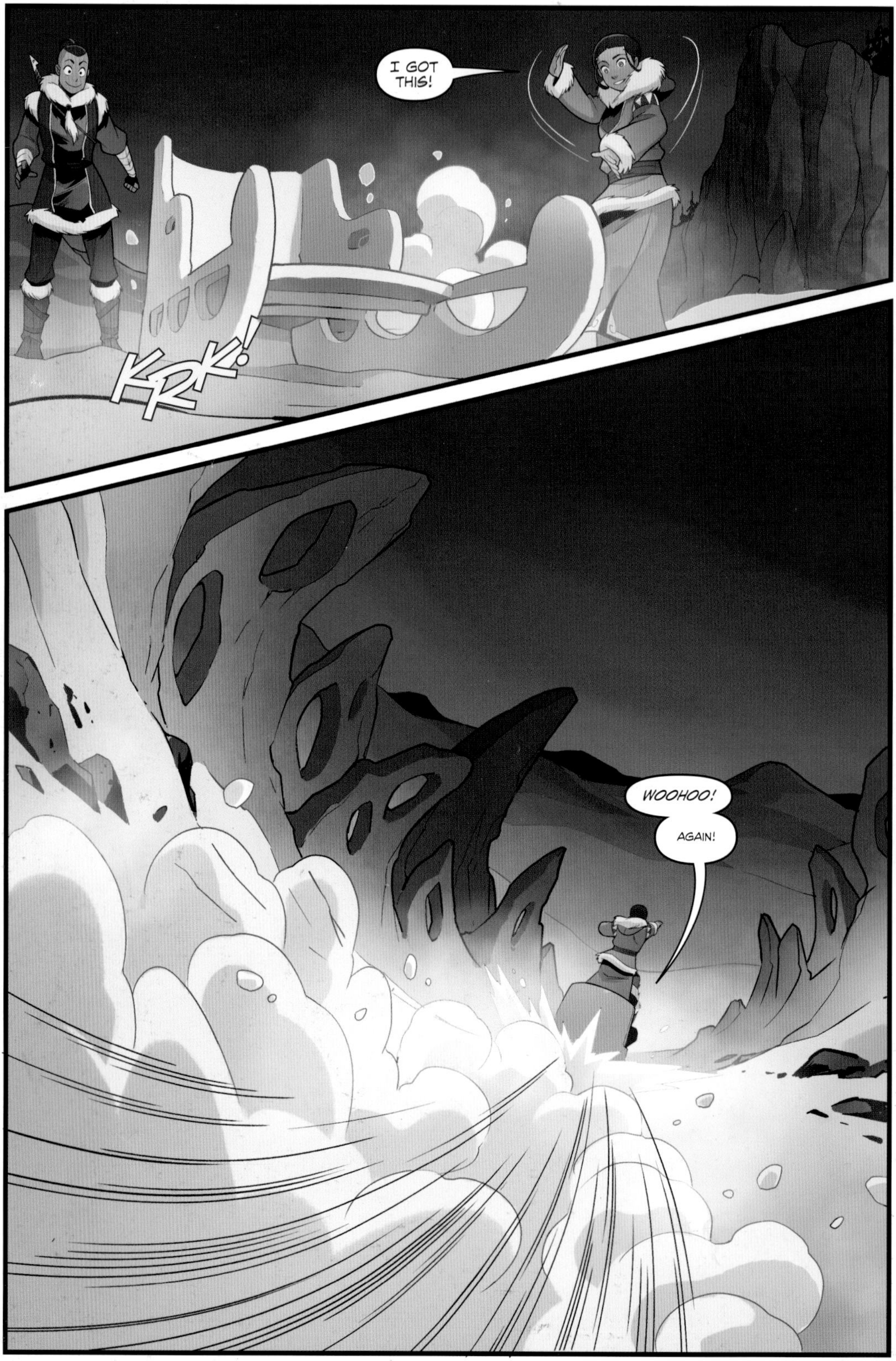
I GOT THIS!
KRK!
WOOHOO!
AGAIN!

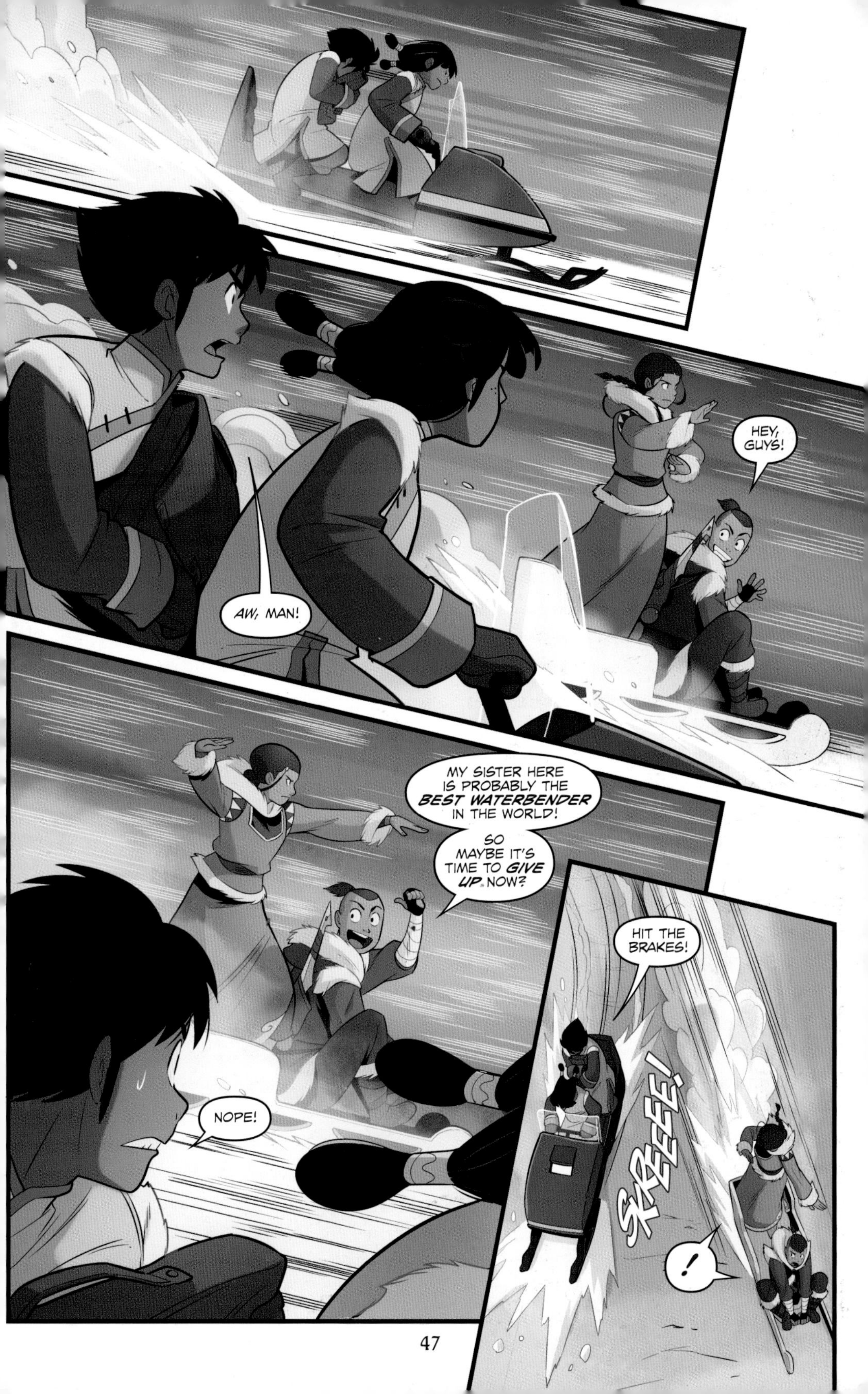
HEY, GUYS!
AW, MAN!
MY SISTER HERE IS PROBABLY THE **BEST WATERBENDER** IN THE WORLD!
SO MAYBE IT'S TIME TO ***GIVE UP*** NOW?
NOPE!
HIT THE BRAKES!
SKREEEEE!
!

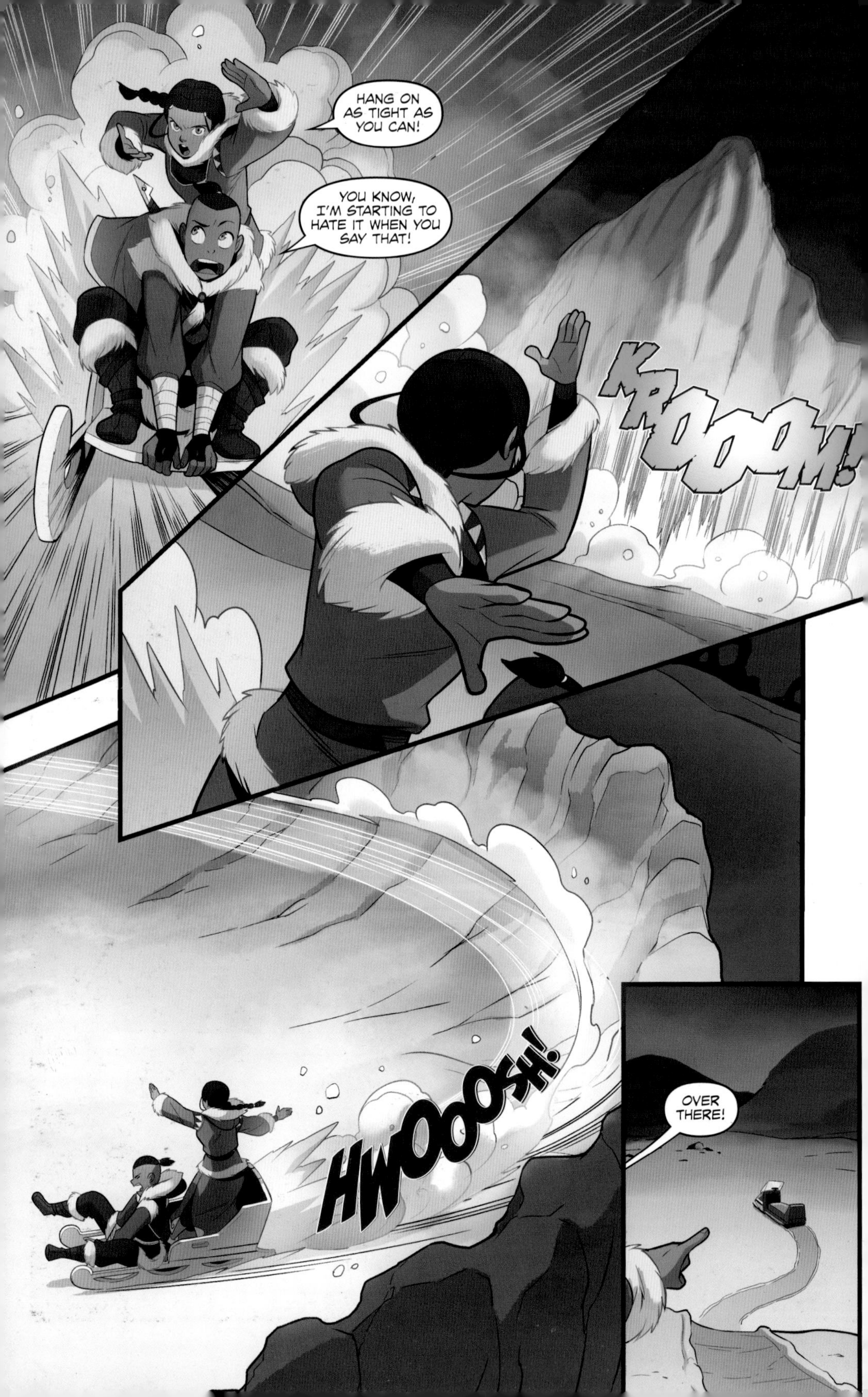
HANG ON AS TIGHT AS YOU CAN!
YOU KNOW, I'M STARTING TO HATE IT WHEN YOU SAY THAT!
KROOOM!
HWOOOSH!
OVER THERE!

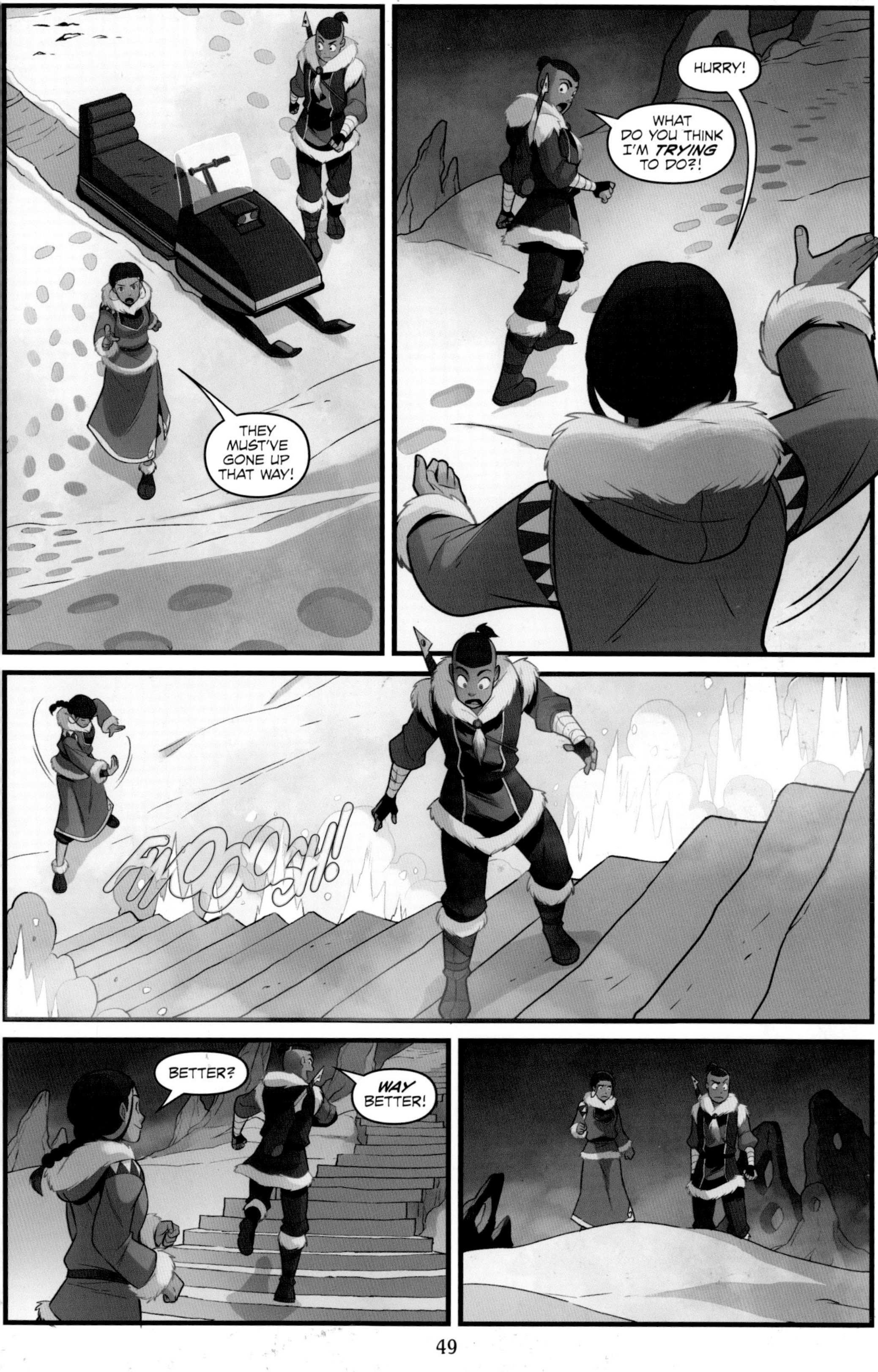
THEY MUST'VE GONE UP THAT WAY!
HURRY!
WHAT DO YOU THINK I'M *TRYING* TO DO?!
FWOOOSH!
BETTER?
WAY BETTER!

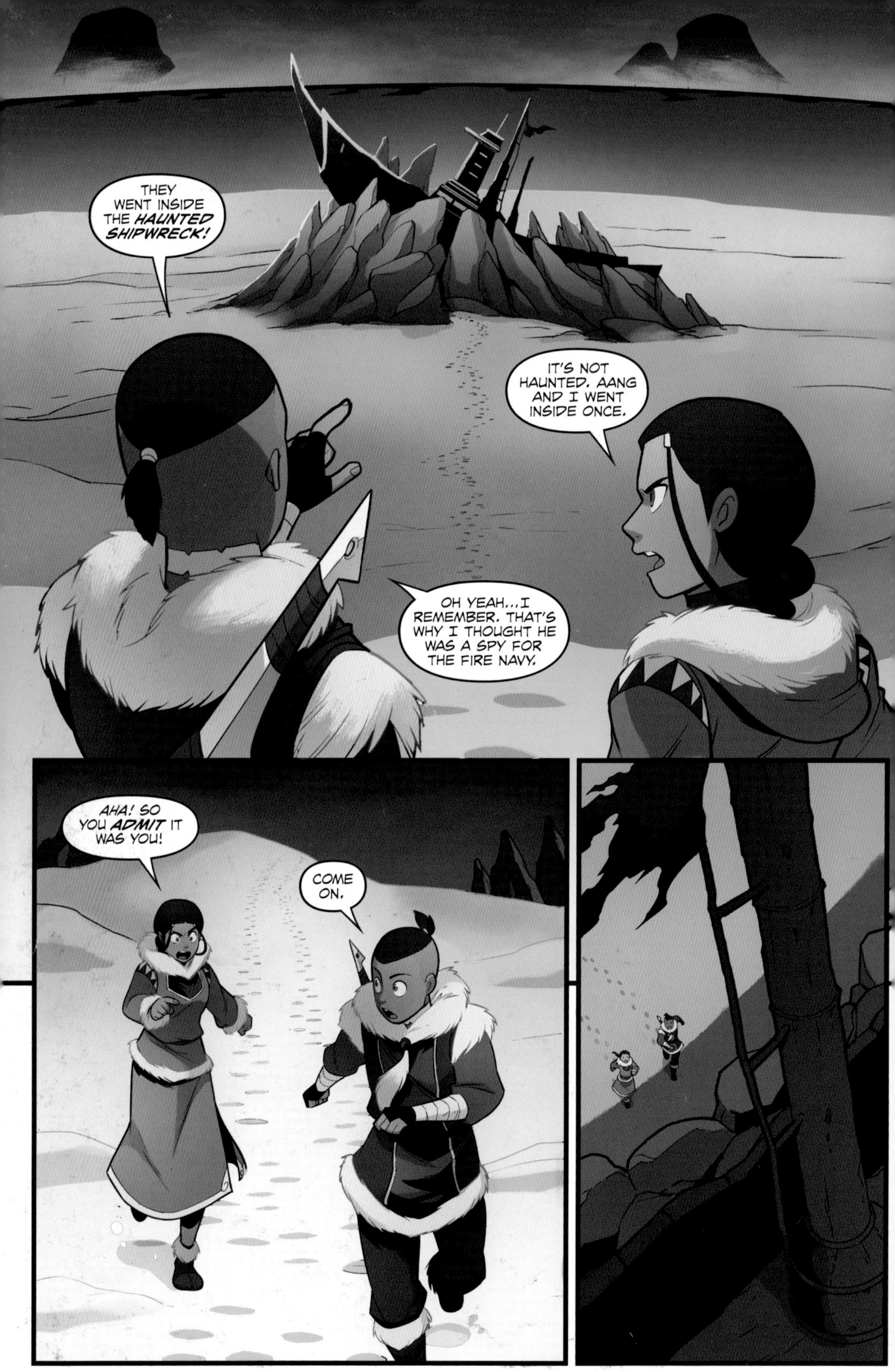
THEY WENT INSIDE THE *HAUNTED SHIPWRECK!*
IT'S NOT HAUNTED. AANG AND I WENT INSIDE ONCE.
OH YEAH...I REMEMBER. THAT'S WHY I THOUGHT HE WAS A SPY FOR THE FIRE NAVY.
AHA! SO YOU *ADMIT* IT WAS YOU!
COME ON.

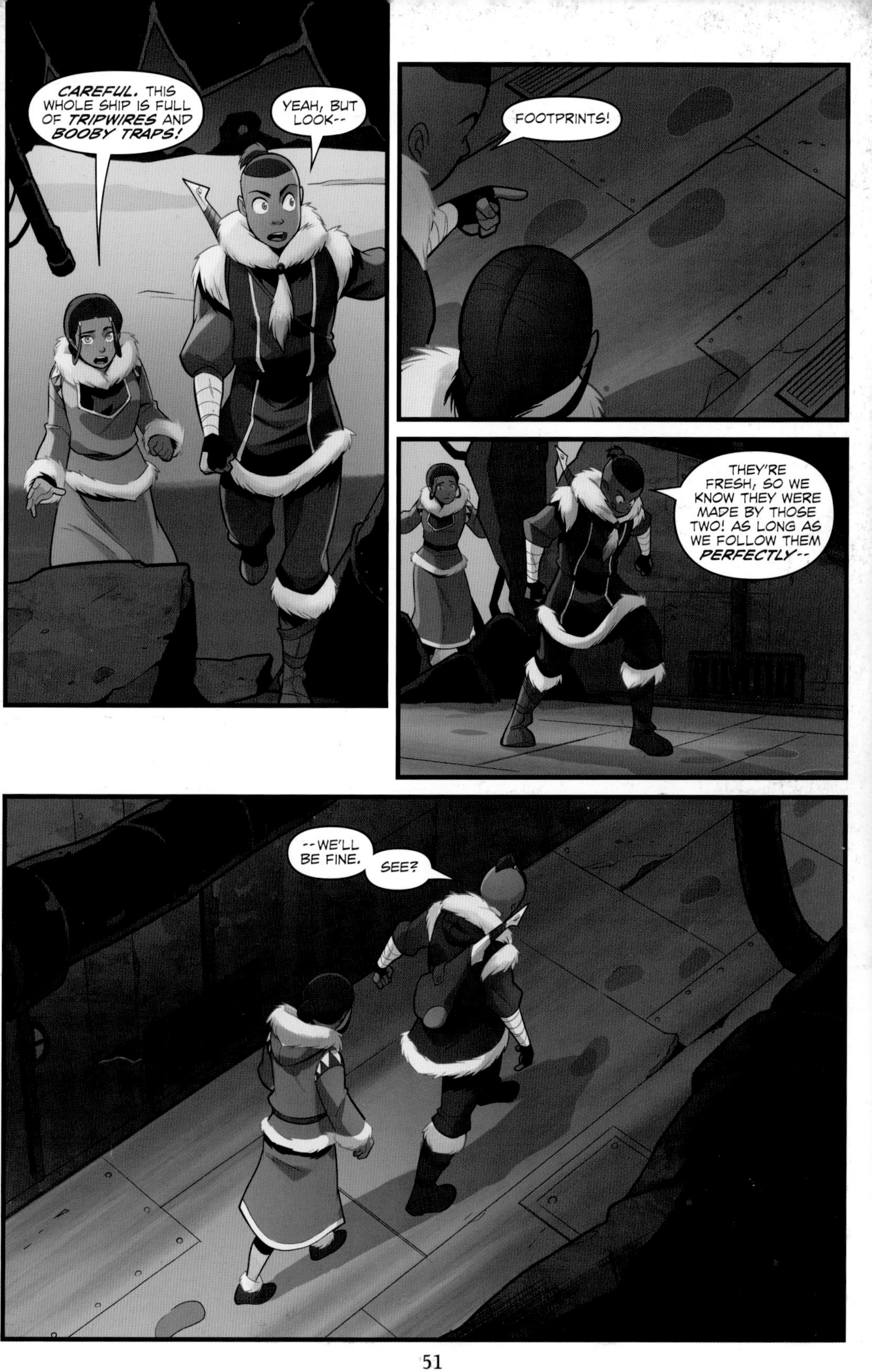
CAREFUL. THIS WHOLE SHIP IS FULL OF TRIPWIRES AND BOOBY TRAPS!
YEAH, BUT LOOK--
FOOTPRINTS!
THEY'RE FRESH, SO WE KNOW THEY WERE MADE BY THOSE TWO! AS LONG AS WE FOLLOW THEM PERFECTLY--
--WE'LL BE FINE.
SEE?

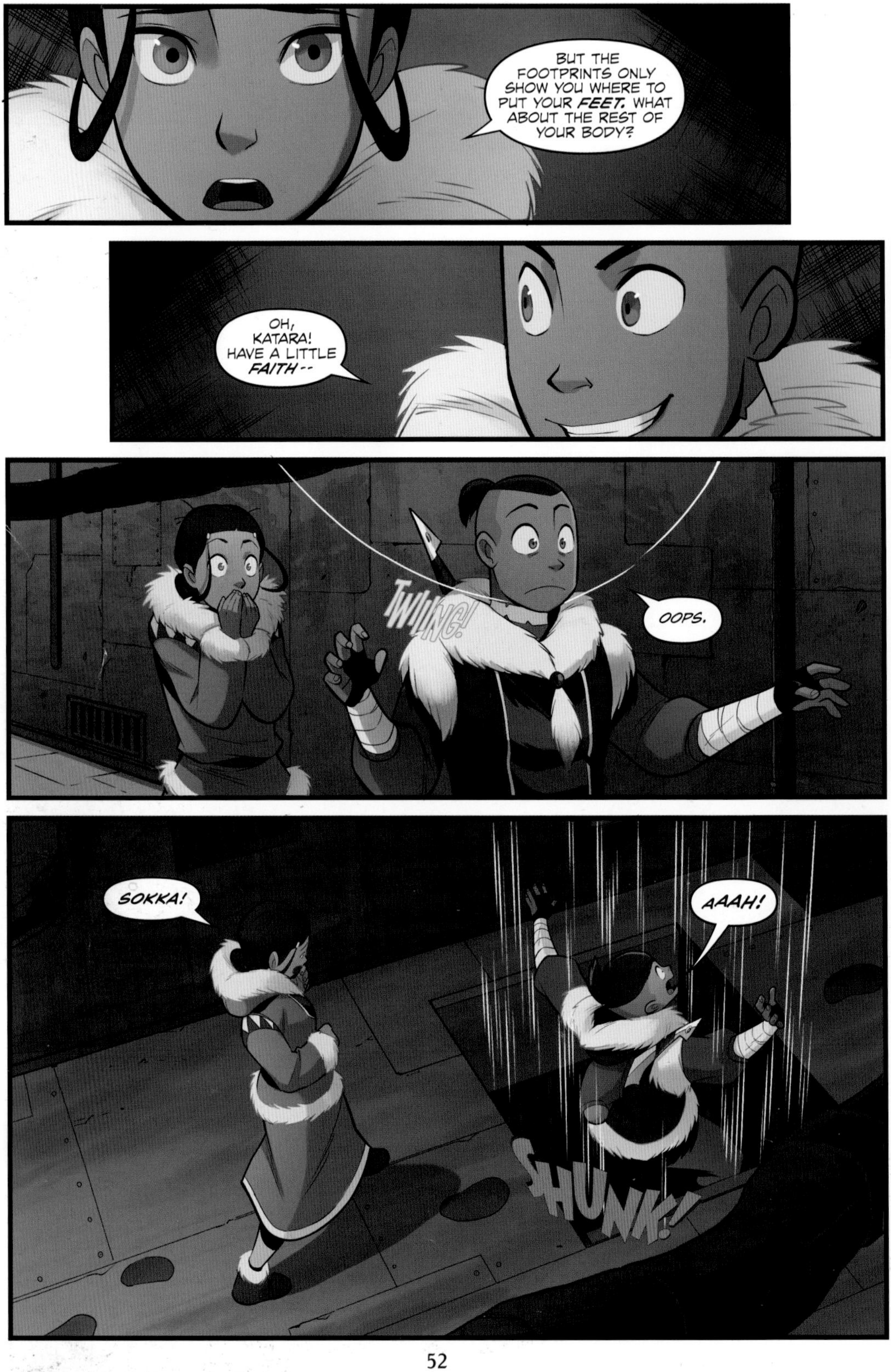
BUT THE FOOTPRINTS ONLY SHOW YOU WHERE TO PUT YOUR FEET. WHAT ABOUT THE REST OF YOUR BODY?
OH, KATARA! HAVE A LITTLE FAITH--
TWIIING!
OOPS.
SOKKA!
AAAH!
SHUNK!

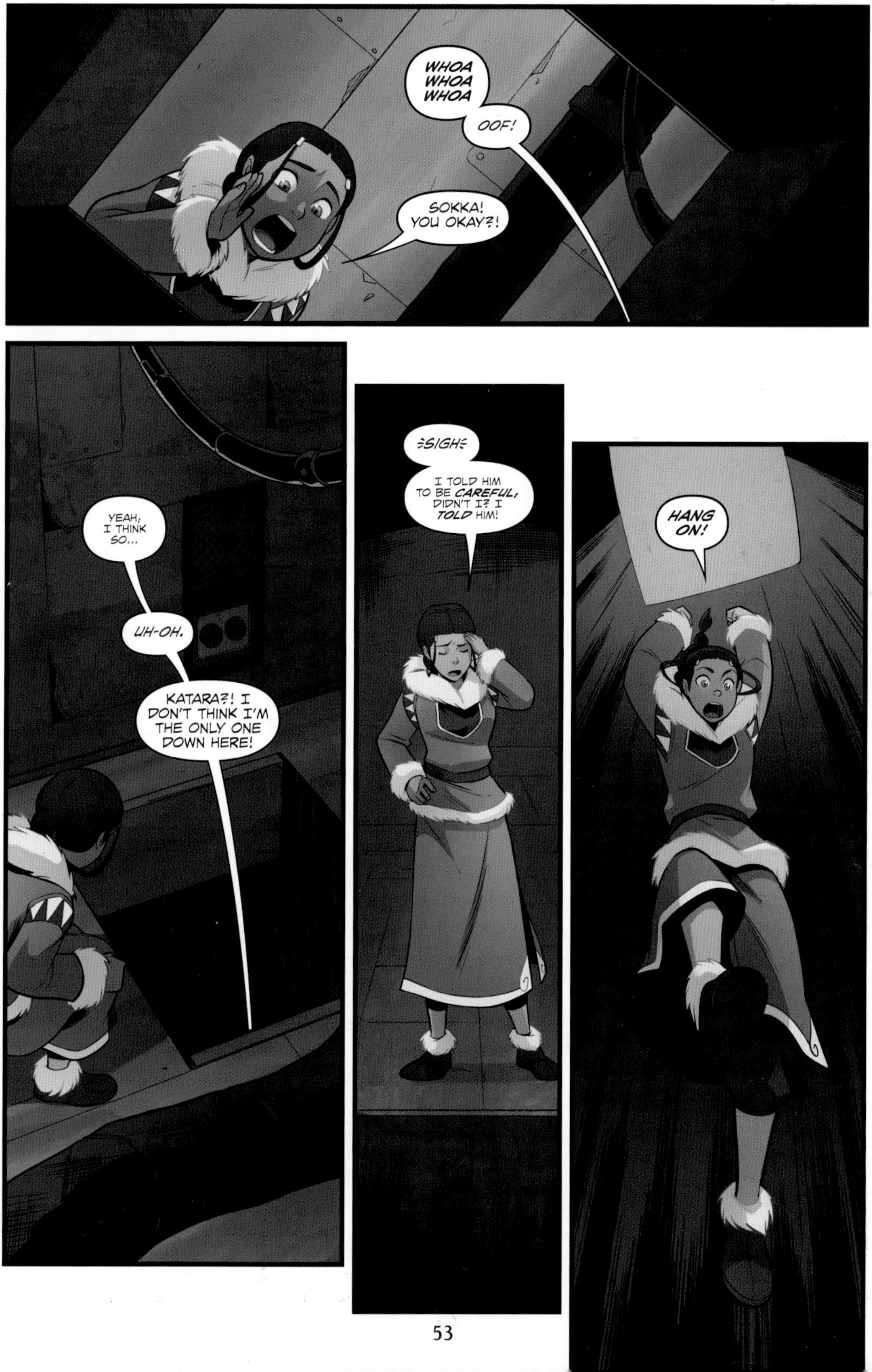
WHOA WHOA WHOA
OOF!
SOKKA! YOU OKAY?!
YEAH, I THINK SO...
UH-OH.
KATARA?! I DON'T THINK I'M THE ONLY ONE DOWN HERE!
SIGH
I TOLD HIM TO BE CAREFUL, DIDN'T I? I TOLD HIM!
HANG ON!

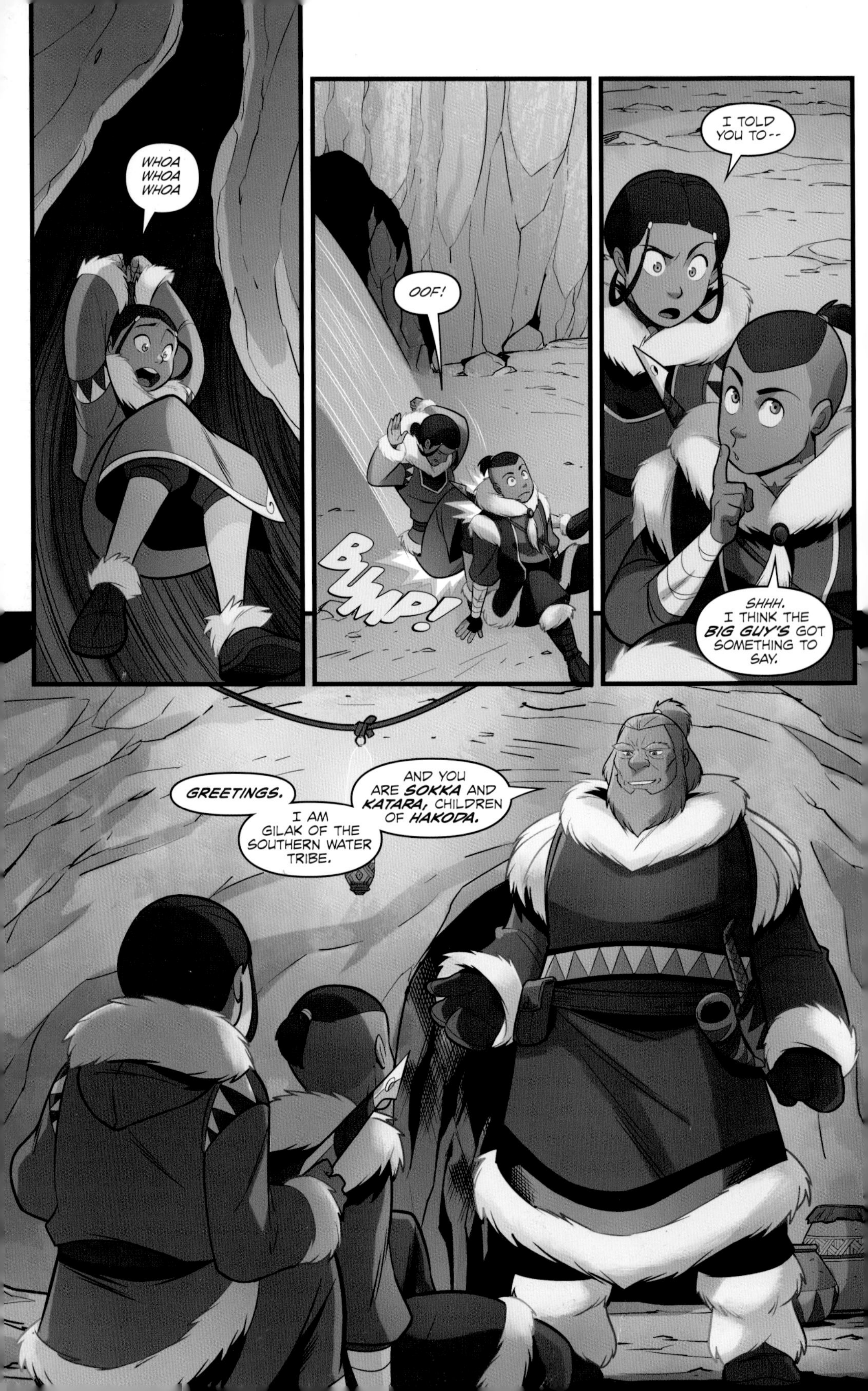
WHOA
WHOA
WHOA
OOF!
BUMP!
I TOLD YOU TO--
SHHH. I THINK THE BIG GUY'S GOT SOMETHING TO SAY.
GREETINGS.
I AM GILAK OF THE SOUTHERN WATER TRIBE.
AND YOU ARE SOKKA AND KATARA, CHILDREN OF HAKODA.

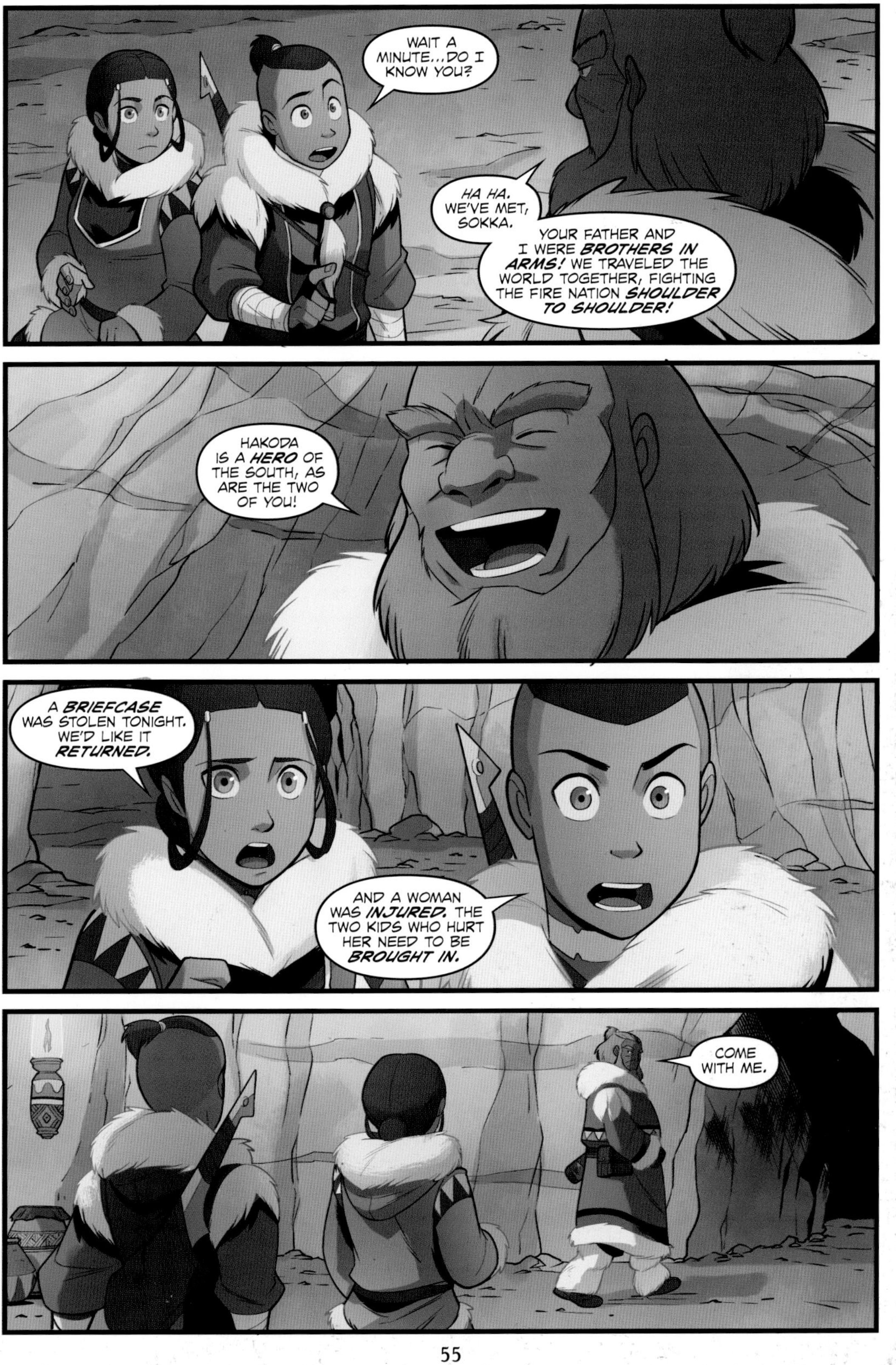
WAIT A MINUTE...DO I KNOW YOU?
HA HA. WE'VE MET, SOKKA.
YOUR FATHER AND I WERE BROTHERS IN ARMS! WE TRAVELED THE WORLD TOGETHER, FIGHTING THE FIRE NATION SHOULDER TO SHOULDER!
HAKODA IS A HERO OF THE SOUTH, AS ARE THE TWO OF YOU!
A BRIEFCASE WAS STOLEN TONIGHT. WE'D LIKE IT RETURNED.
AND A WOMAN WAS INJURED. THE TWO KIDS WHO HURT HER NEED TO BE BROUGHT IN.
COME WITH ME.

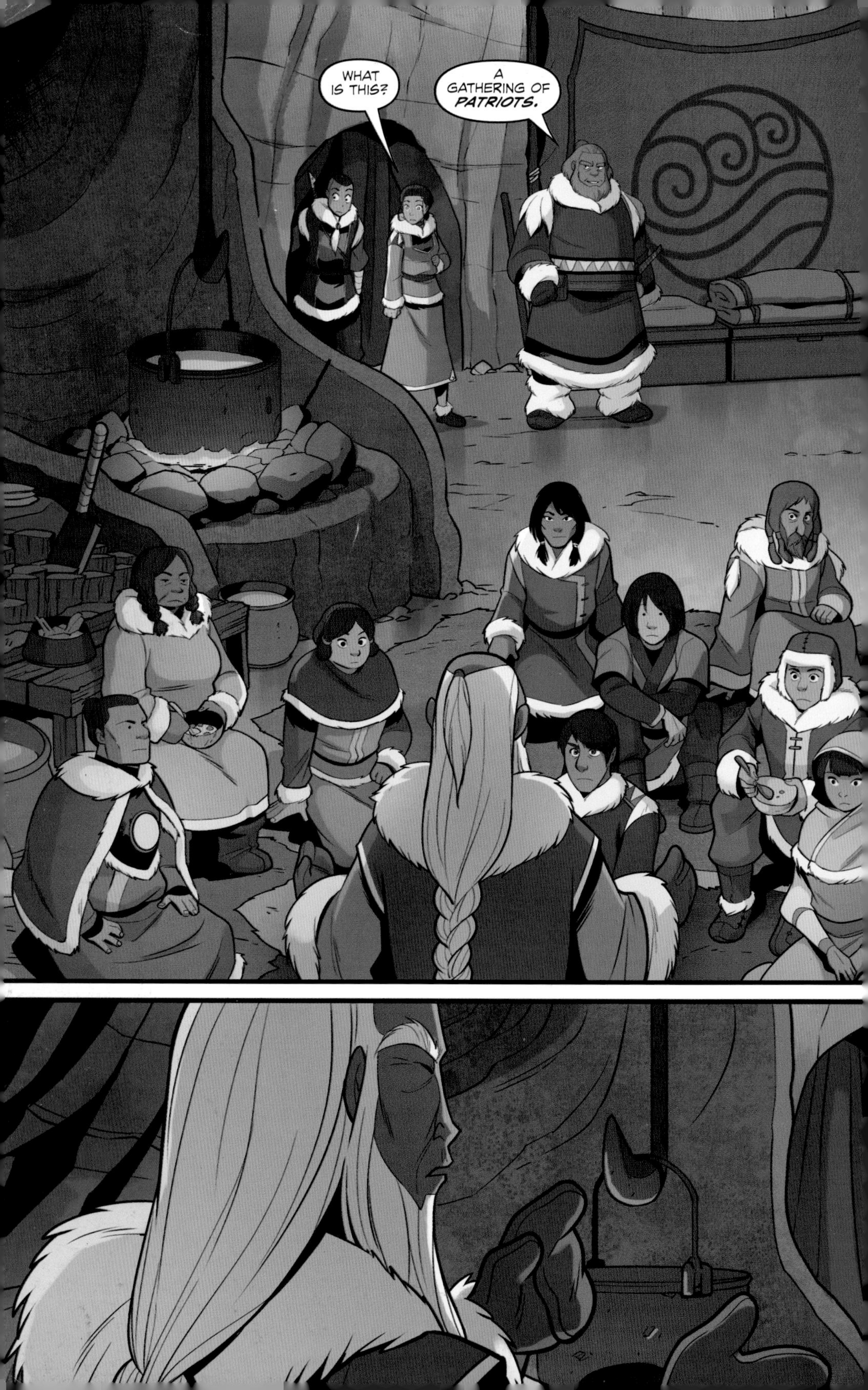
WHAT IS THIS?
A GATHERING OF PATRIOTS.

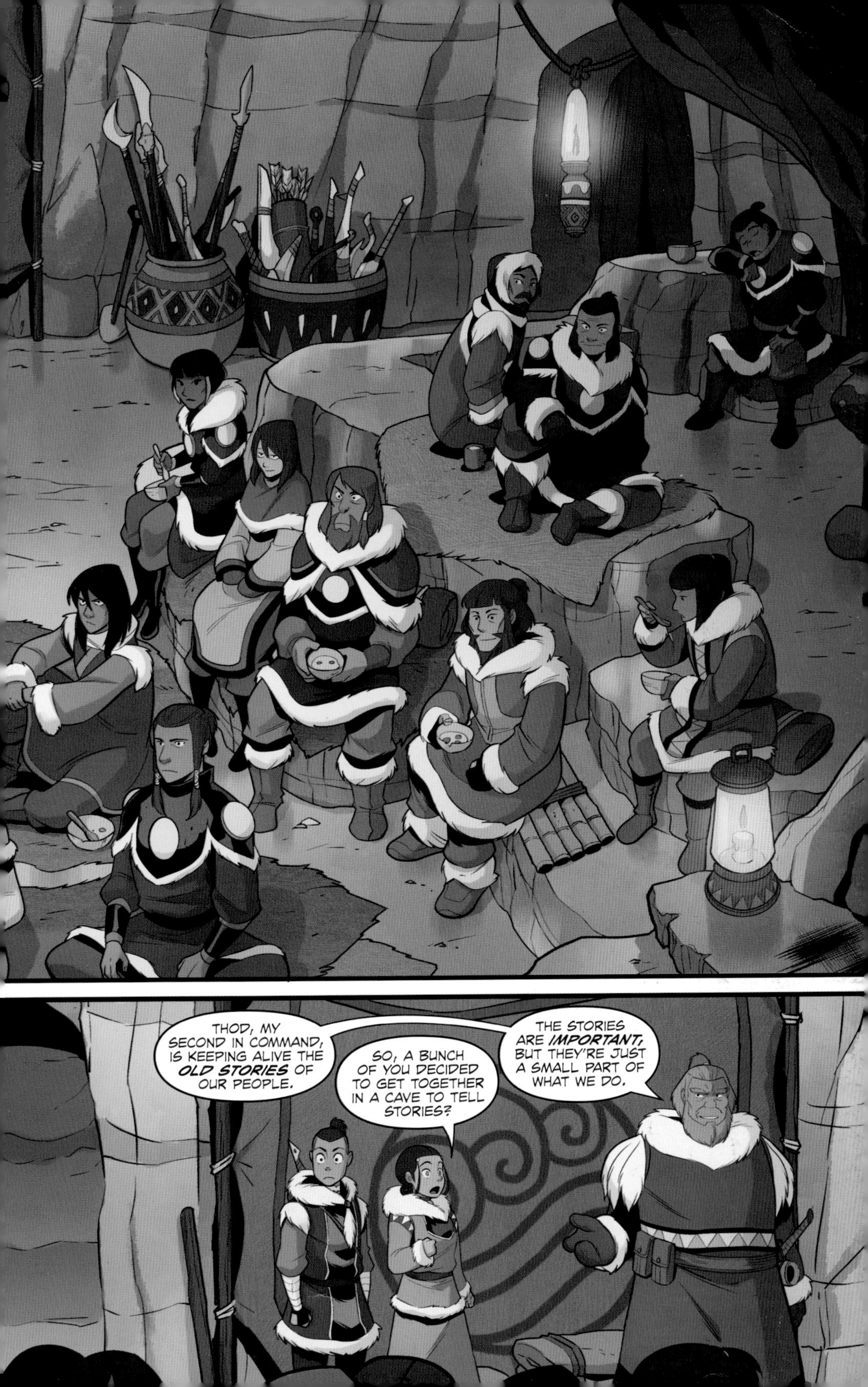
THOD, MY SECOND IN COMMAND, IS KEEPING ALIVE THE OLD STORIES OF OUR PEOPLE.
SO, A BUNCH OF YOU DECIDED TO GET TOGETHER IN A CAVE TO TELL STORIES?
THE STORIES ARE IMPORTANT, BUT THEY'RE JUST A SMALL PART OF WHAT WE DO.

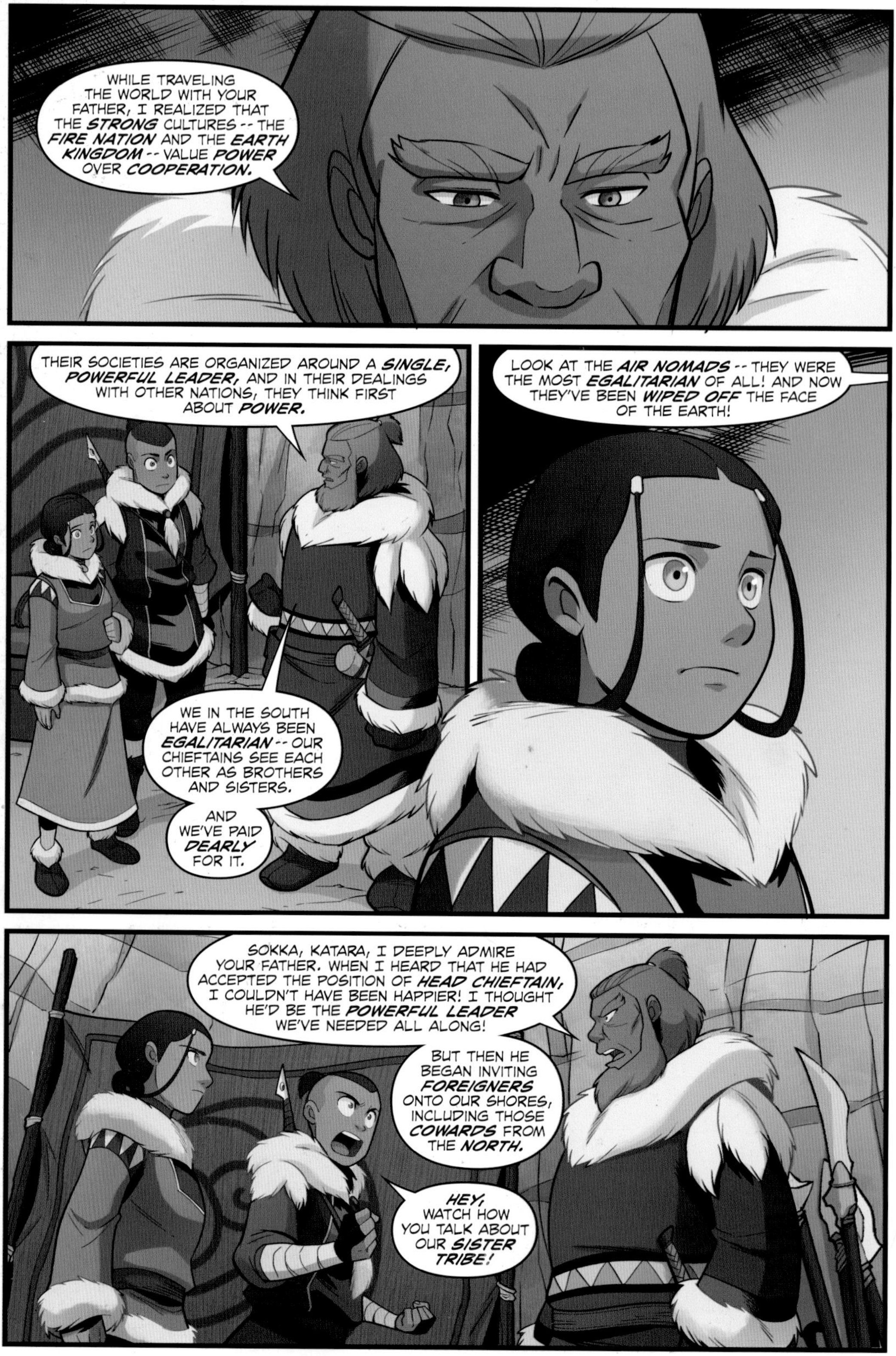
WHILE TRAVELING THE WORLD WITH YOUR FATHER, I REALIZED THAT THE STRONG CULTURES -- THE FIRE NATION AND THE EARTH KINGDOM -- VALUE POWER OVER COOPERATION.
THEIR SOCIETIES ARE ORGANIZED AROUND A SINGLE, POWERFUL LEADER, AND IN THEIR DEALINGS WITH OTHER NATIONS, THEY THINK FIRST ABOUT POWER.
WE IN THE SOUTH HAVE ALWAYS BEEN EGALITARIAN -- OUR CHIEFTAINS SEE EACH OTHER AS BROTHERS AND SISTERS.
AND WE'VE PAID DEARLY FOR IT.
LOOK AT THE AIR NOMADS -- THEY WERE THE MOST EGALITARIAN OF ALL! AND NOW THEY'VE BEEN WIPED OFF THE FACE OF THE EARTH!
SOKKA, KATARA, I DEEPLY ADMIRE YOUR FATHER. WHEN I HEARD THAT HE HAD ACCEPTED THE POSITION OF HEAD CHIEFTAIN, I COULDN'T HAVE BEEN HAPPIER! I THOUGHT HE'D BE THE POWERFUL LEADER WE'VE NEEDED ALL ALONG!
BUT THEN HE BEGAN INVITING FOREIGNERS ONTO OUR SHORES, INCLUDING THOSE COWARDS FROM THE NORTH.
HEY, WATCH HOW YOU TALK ABOUT OUR SISTER TRIBE!

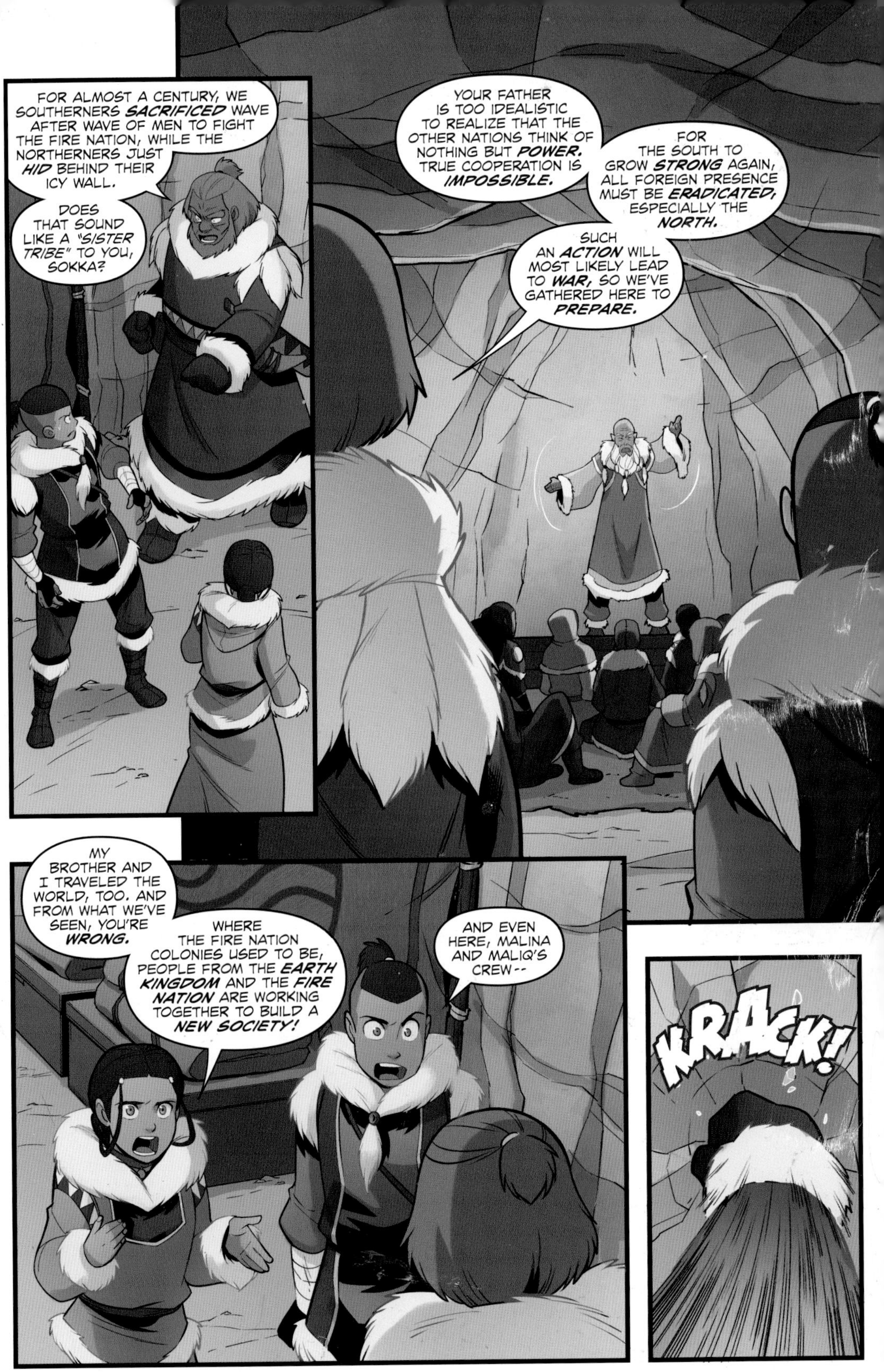
FOR ALMOST A CENTURY, WE SOUTHERNERS SACRIFICED WAVE AFTER WAVE OF MEN TO FIGHT THE FIRE NATION, WHILE THE NORTHERNERS JUST HID BEHIND THEIR ICY WALL.
DOES THAT SOUND LIKE A "SISTER TRIBE" TO YOU, SOKKA?
YOUR FATHER IS TOO IDEALISTIC TO REALIZE THAT THE OTHER NATIONS THINK OF NOTHING BUT POWER. TRUE COOPERATION IS IMPOSSIBLE.
FOR THE SOUTH TO GROW STRONG AGAIN, ALL FOREIGN PRESENCE MUST BE ERADICATED, ESPECIALLY THE NORTH.
SUCH AN ACTION WILL MOST LIKELY LEAD TO WAR, SO WE'VE GATHERED HERE TO PREPARE.
MY BROTHER AND I TRAVELED THE WORLD, TOO. AND FROM WHAT WE'VE SEEN, YOU'RE WRONG.
WHERE THE FIRE NATION COLONIES USED TO BE, PEOPLE FROM THE EARTH KINGDOM AND THE FIRE NATION ARE WORKING TOGETHER TO BUILD A NEW SOCIETY!
AND EVEN HERE, MALINA AND MALIQ'S CREW--
KRACK!

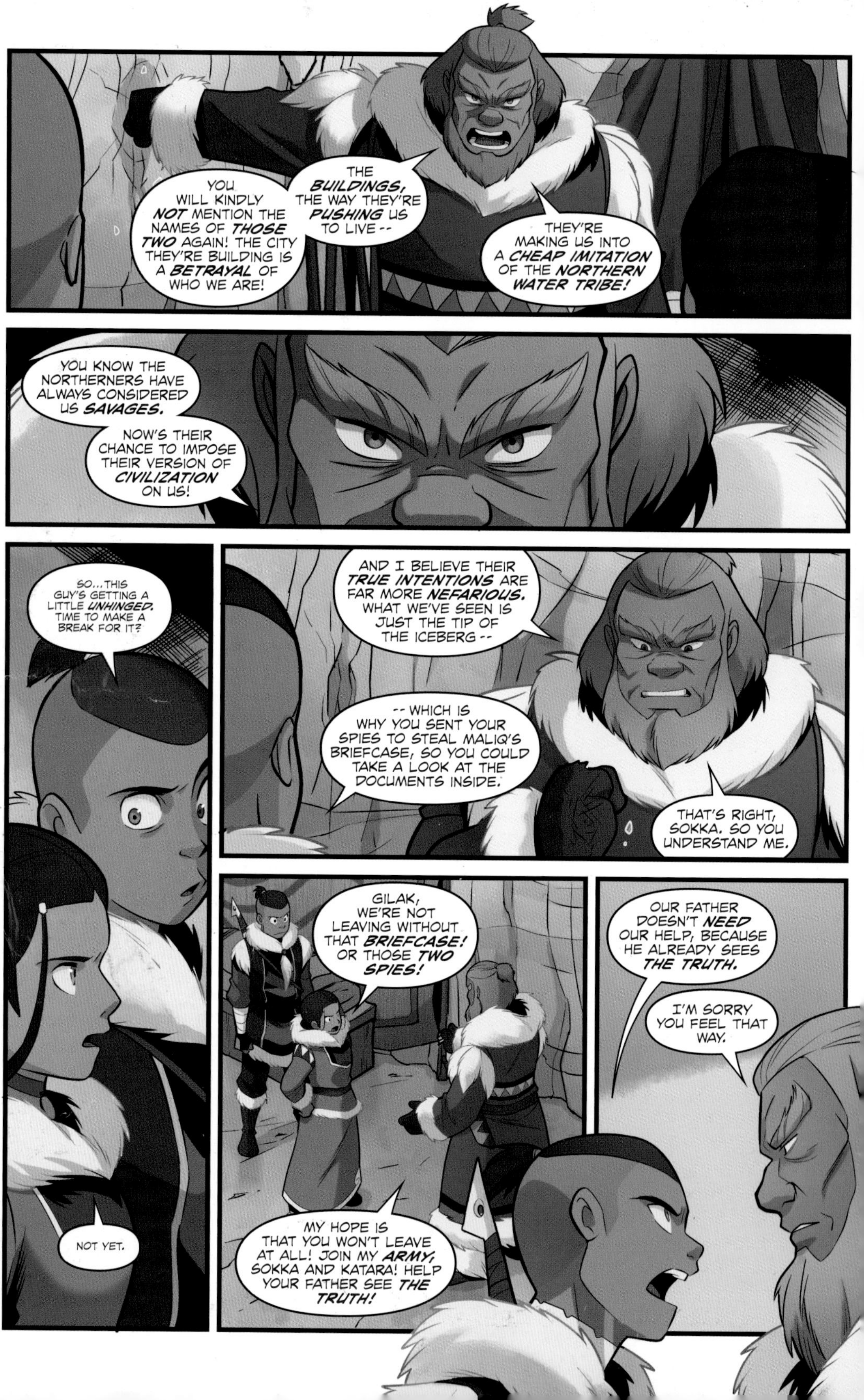

YOU WILL KINDLY NOT MENTION THE NAMES OF THOSE TWO AGAIN! THE CITY THEY'RE BUILDING IS A BETRAYAL OF WHO WE ARE!
THE BUILDINGS, THE WAY THEY'RE PUSHING US TO LIVE --
THEY'RE MAKING US INTO A CHEAP IMITATION OF THE NORTHERN WATER TRIBE!
YOU KNOW THE NORTHERNERS HAVE ALWAYS CONSIDERED US SAVAGES.
NOW'S THEIR CHANCE TO IMPOSE THEIR VERSION OF CIVILIZATION ON US!
SO...THIS GUY'S GETTING A LITTLE UNHINGED. TIME TO MAKE A BREAK FOR IT?
NOT YET.
AND I BELIEVE THEIR TRUE INTENTIONS ARE FAR MORE NEFARIOUS. WHAT WE'VE SEEN IS JUST THE TIP OF THE ICEBERG --
-- WHICH IS WHY YOU SENT YOUR SPIES TO STEAL MALIQ'S BRIEFCASE, SO YOU COULD TAKE A LOOK AT THE DOCUMENTS INSIDE.
THAT'S RIGHT, SOKKA. SO YOU UNDERSTAND ME.
GILAK, WE'RE NOT LEAVING WITHOUT THAT BRIEFCASE! OR THOSE TWO SPIES!
MY HOPE IS THAT YOU WON'T LEAVE AT ALL! JOIN MY ARMY, SOKKA AND KATARA! HELP YOUR FATHER SEE THE TRUTH!
OUR FATHER DOESN'T NEED OUR HELP, BECAUSE HE ALREADY SEES THE TRUTH.
I'M SORRY YOU FEEL THAT WAY.

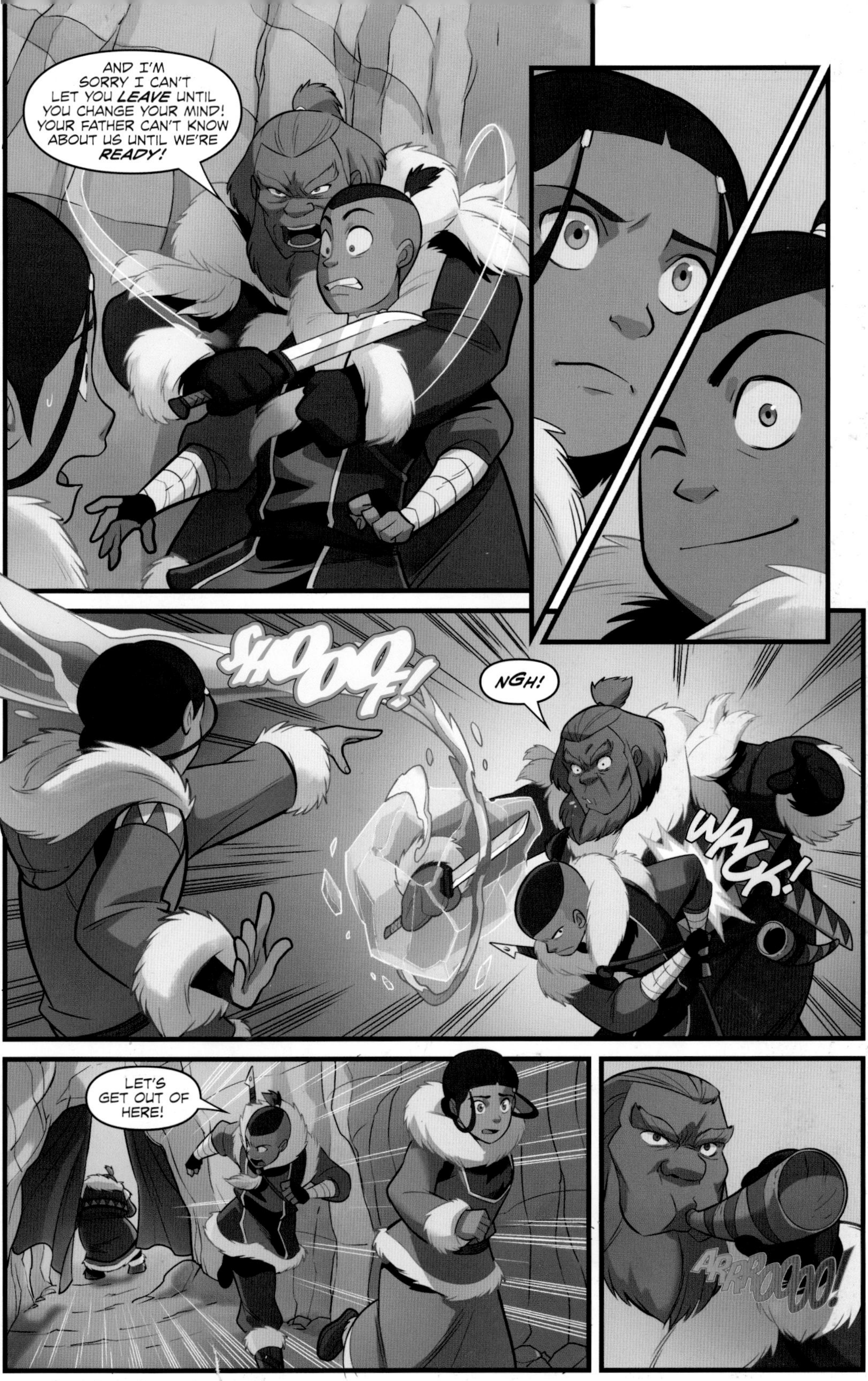
AND I'M SORRY I CAN'T LET YOU LEAVE UNTIL YOU CHANGE YOUR MIND! YOUR FATHER CAN'T KNOW ABOUT US UNTIL WE'RE READY!
SHOOOK!
NGH!
WACK!
LET'S GET OUT OF HERE!
ARRROOOOO!

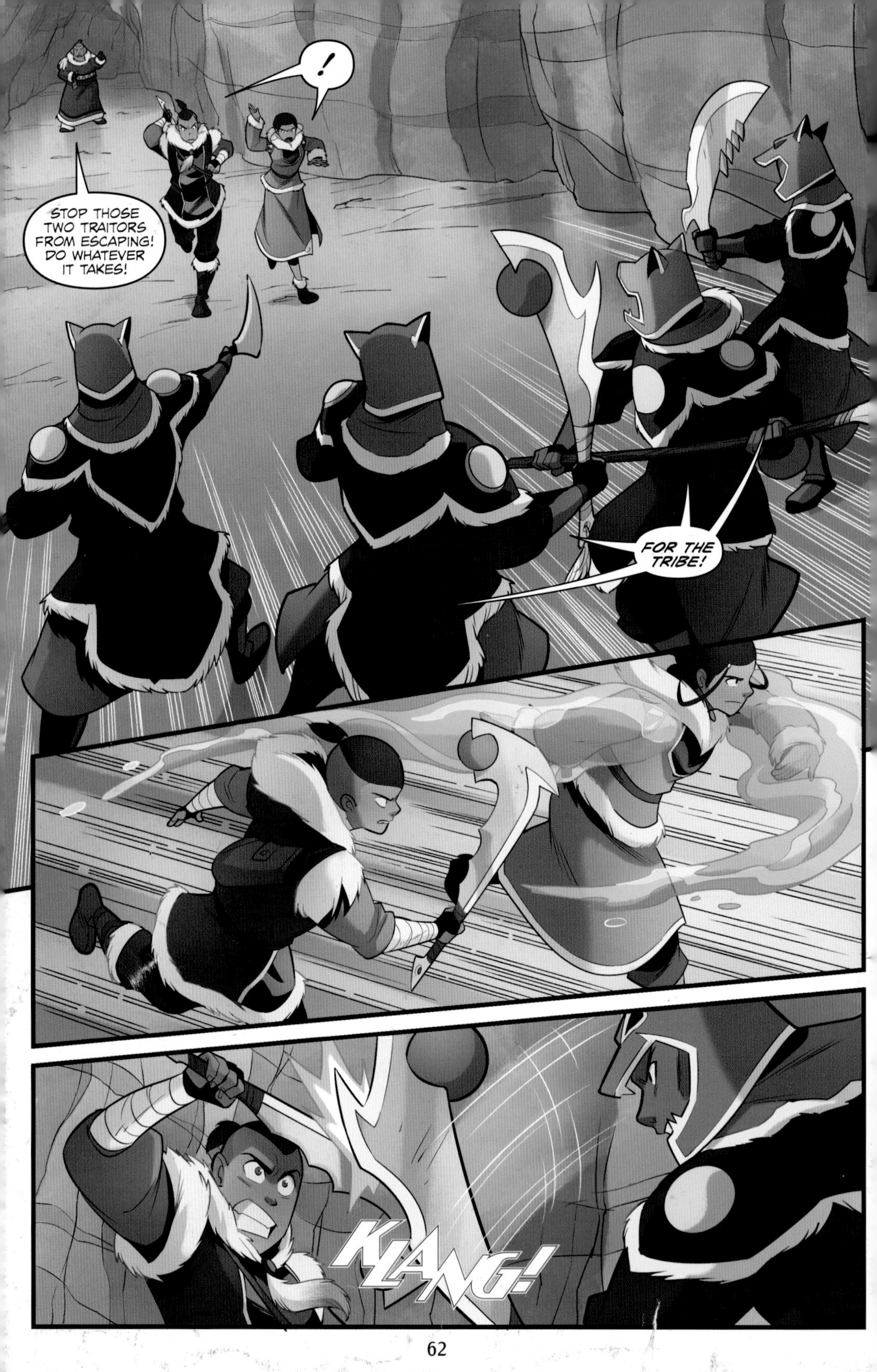
!
STOP THOSE TWO TRAITORS FROM ESCAPING! DO WHATEVER IT TAKES!
FOR THE TRIBE!
KLANG!

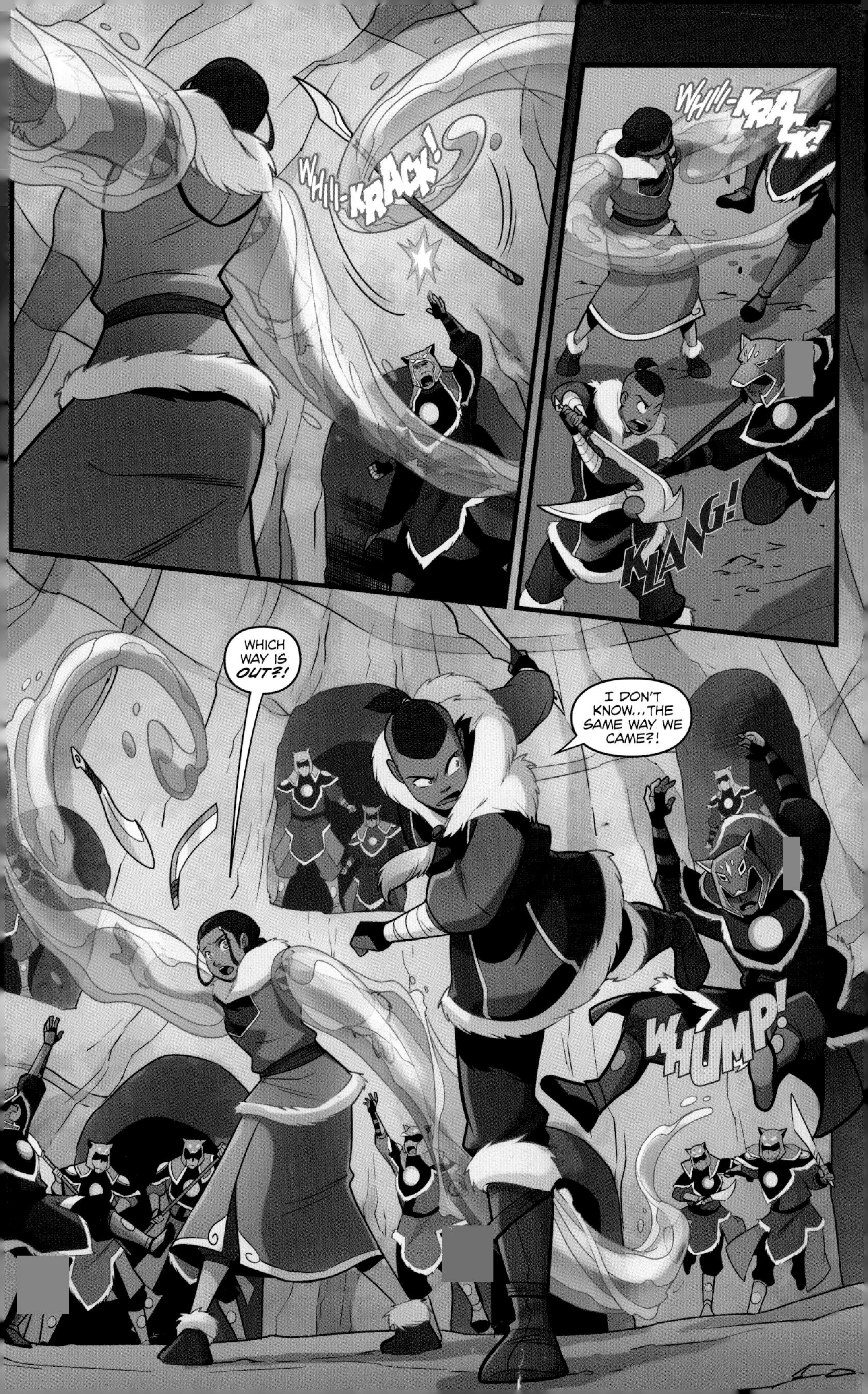
WHIII-KRACK!
WHIII-KRACK!
KLANG!
WHICH WAY IS OUT?!
I DON'T KNOW... THE SAME WAY WE CAME?!
WHUMP!

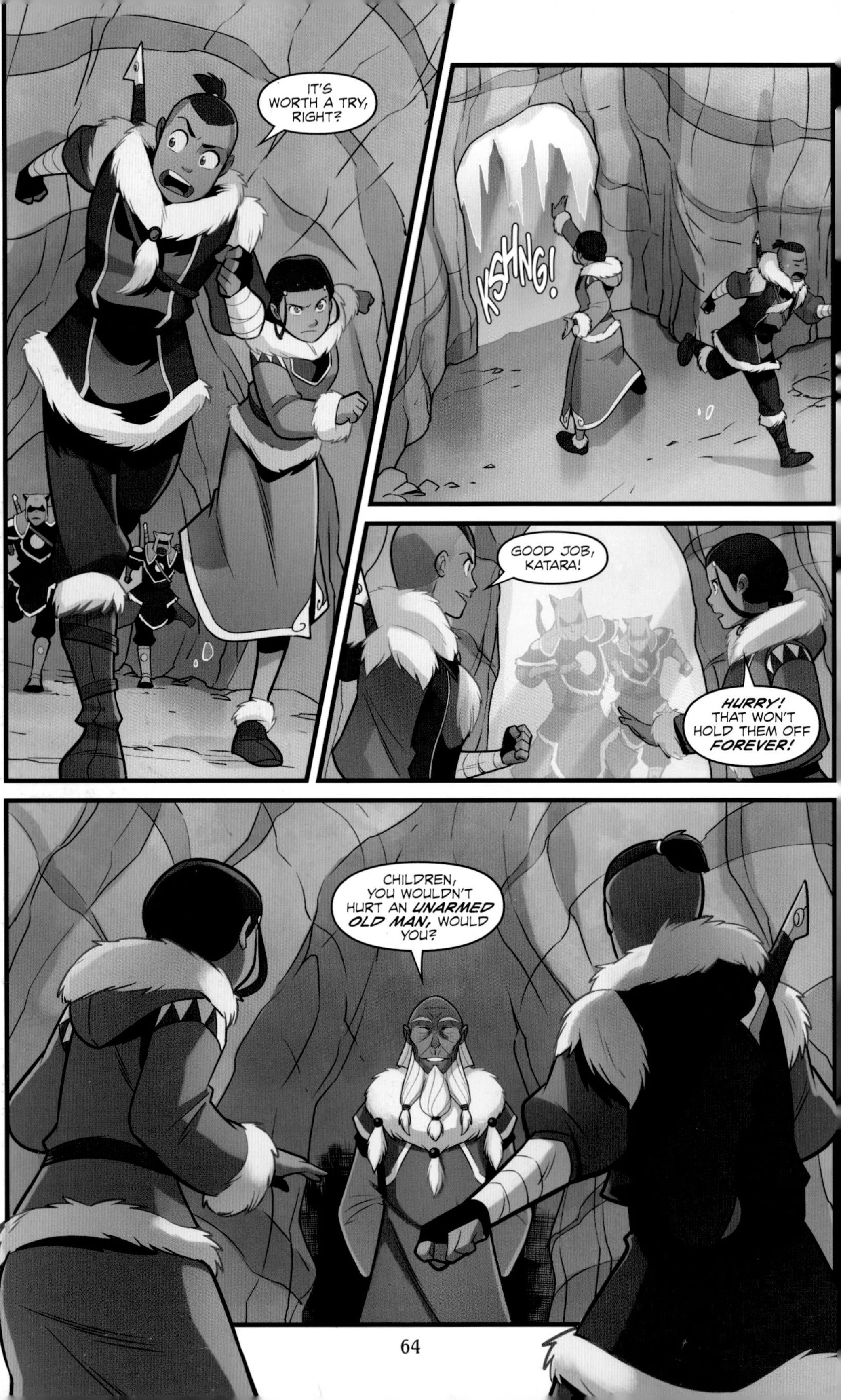
IT'S WORTH A TRY, RIGHT?
KSHNG!
GOOD JOB, KATARA!
HURRY! THAT WON'T HOLD THEM OFF FOREVER!
CHILDREN, YOU WOULDN'T HURT AN UNARMED OLD MAN, WOULD YOU?

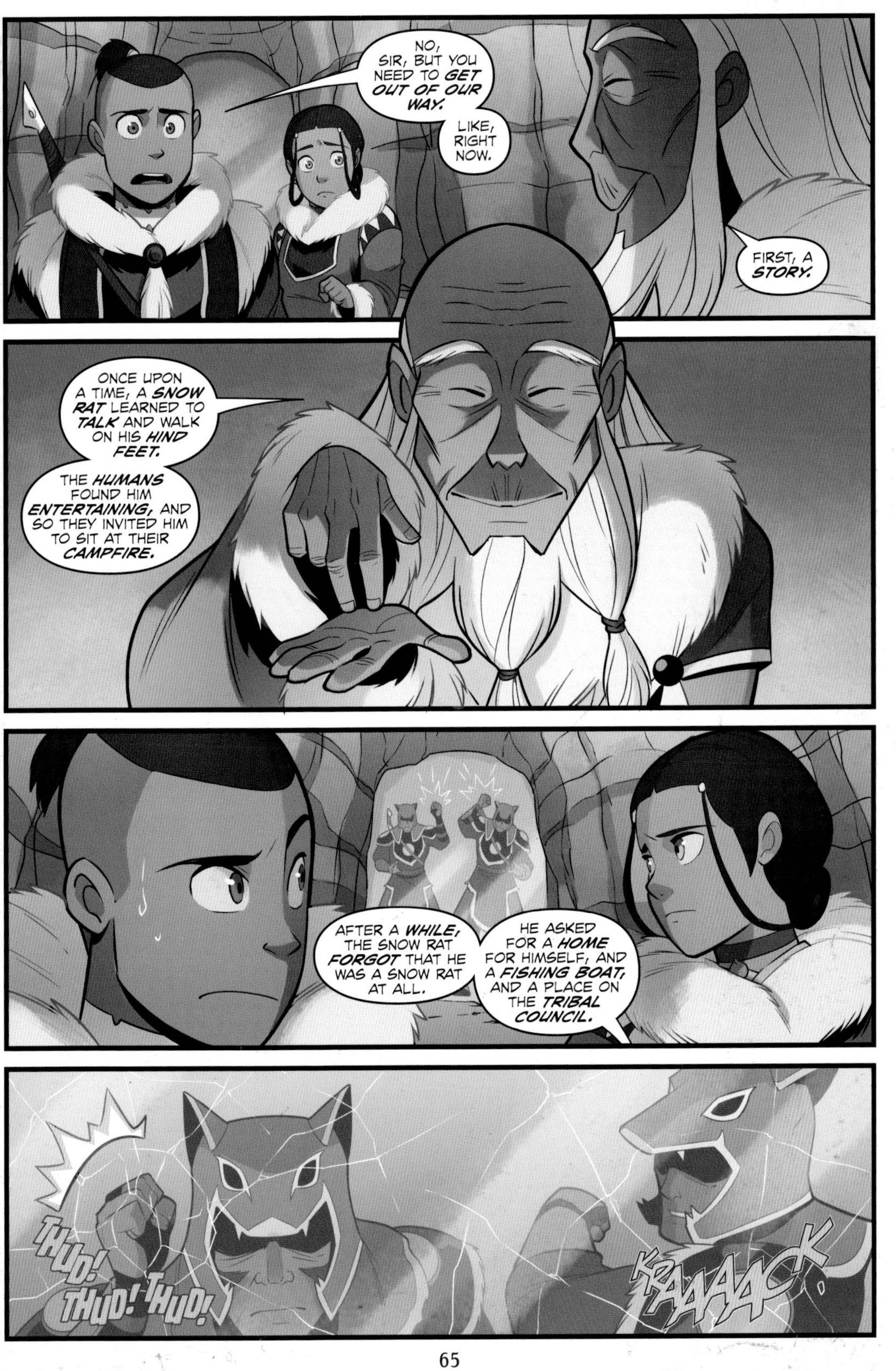
NO, SIR, BUT YOU NEED TO GET OUT OF OUR WAY.
LIKE, RIGHT NOW.
FIRST, A STORY.
ONCE UPON A TIME, A SNOW RAT LEARNED TO TALK AND WALK ON HIS HIND FEET.
THE HUMANS FOUND HIM ENTERTAINING, AND SO THEY INVITED HIM TO SIT AT THEIR CAMPFIRE.
AFTER A WHILE, THE SNOW RAT FORGOT THAT HE WAS A SNOW RAT AT ALL.
HE ASKED FOR A HOME FOR HIMSELF, AND A FISHING BOAT, AND A PLACE ON THE TRIBAL COUNCIL.
THUD! THUD! THUD!
KRAAAACK

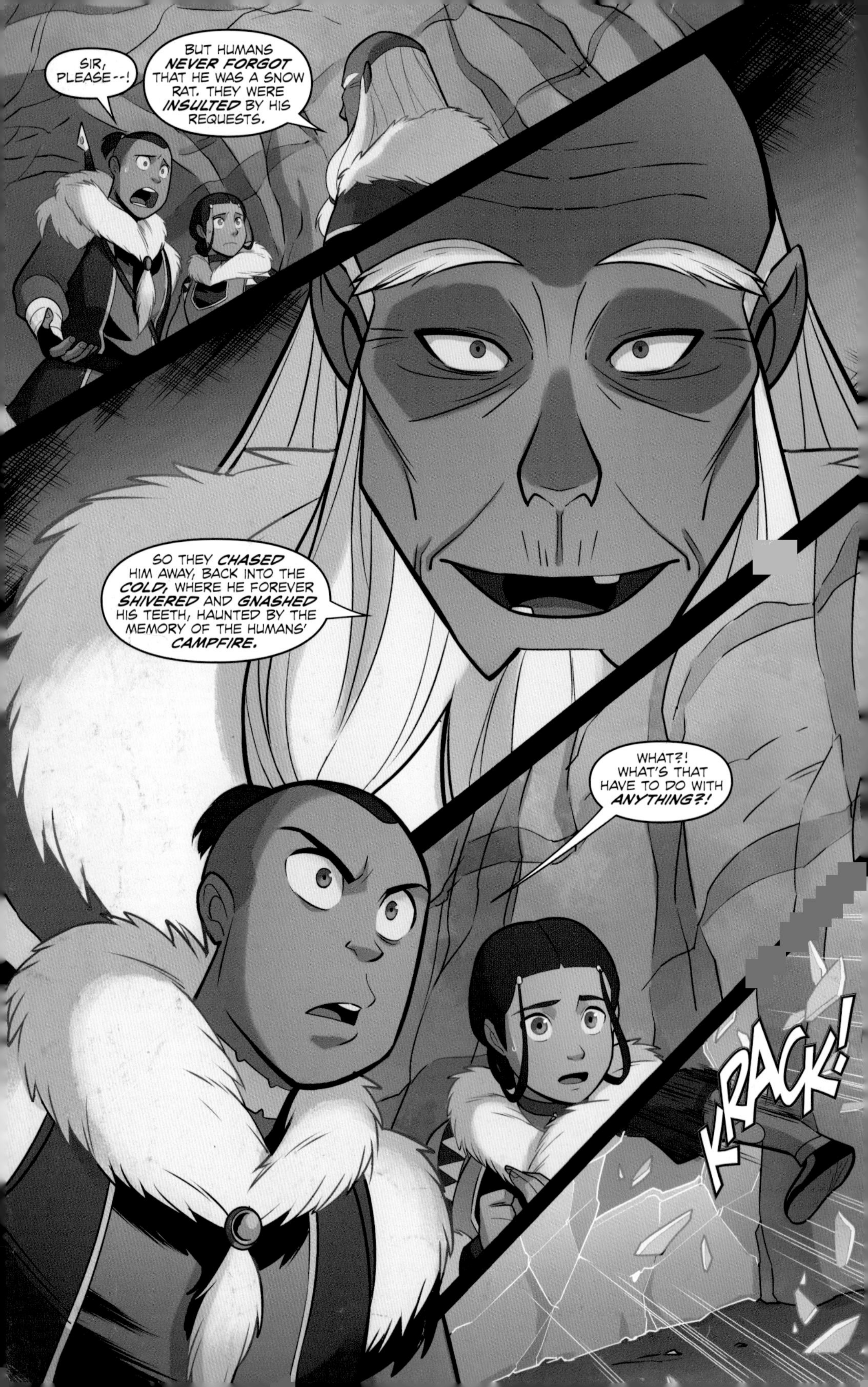
SIR, PLEASE--!
BUT HUMANS NEVER FORGOT THAT HE WAS A SNOW RAT. THEY WERE INSULTED BY HIS REQUESTS.
SO THEY CHASED HIM AWAY, BACK INTO THE COLD, WHERE HE FOREVER SHIVERED AND GNASHED HIS TEETH, HAUNTED BY THE MEMORY OF THE HUMANS' CAMPFIRE.
WHAT?! WHAT'S THAT HAVE TO DO WITH ANYTHING?!
KRACK!

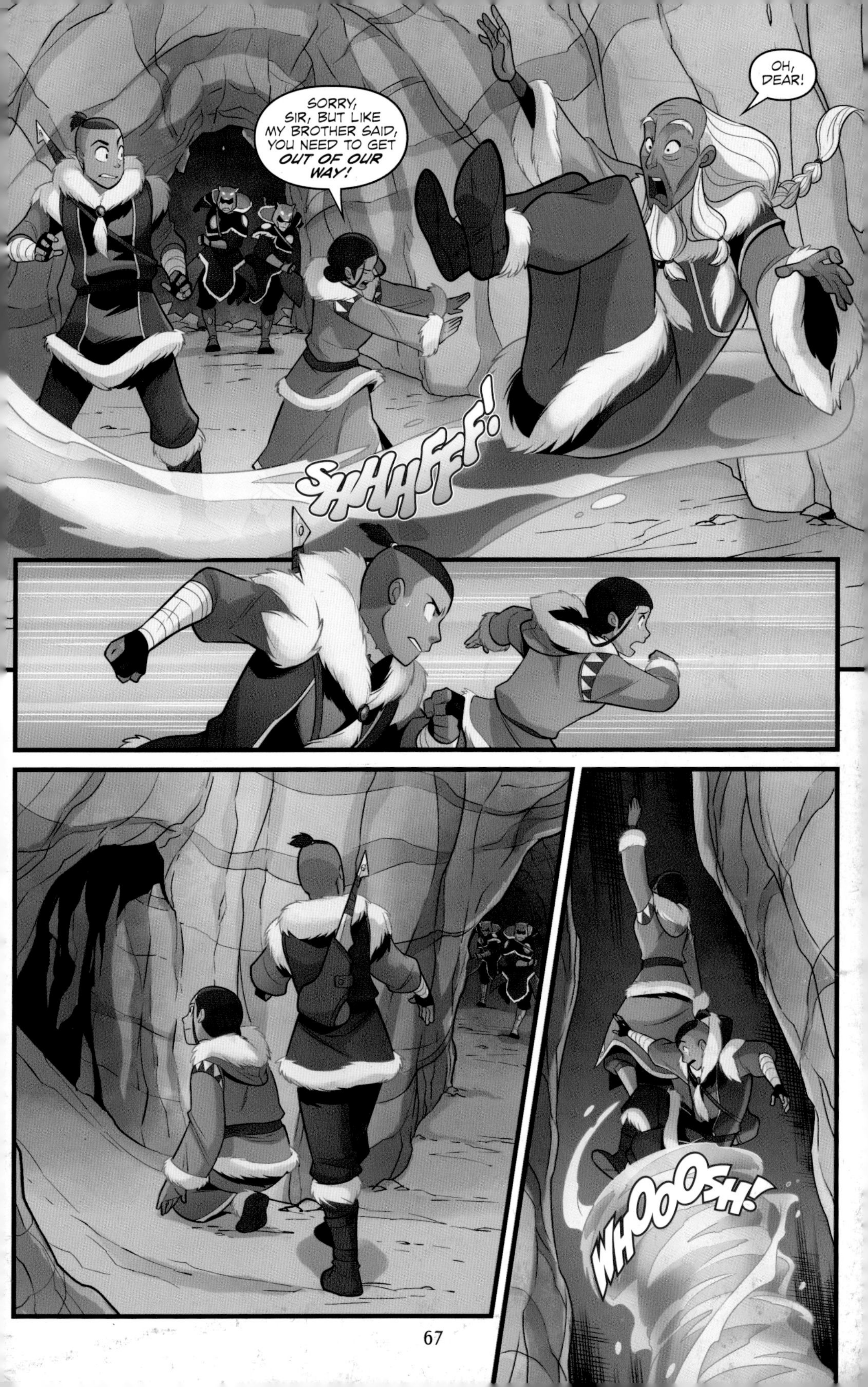
SORRY, SIR, BUT LIKE MY BROTHER SAID, YOU NEED TO GET OUT OF OUR WAY!
OH, DEAR!
SHHHFFF!
WHOOOSH!

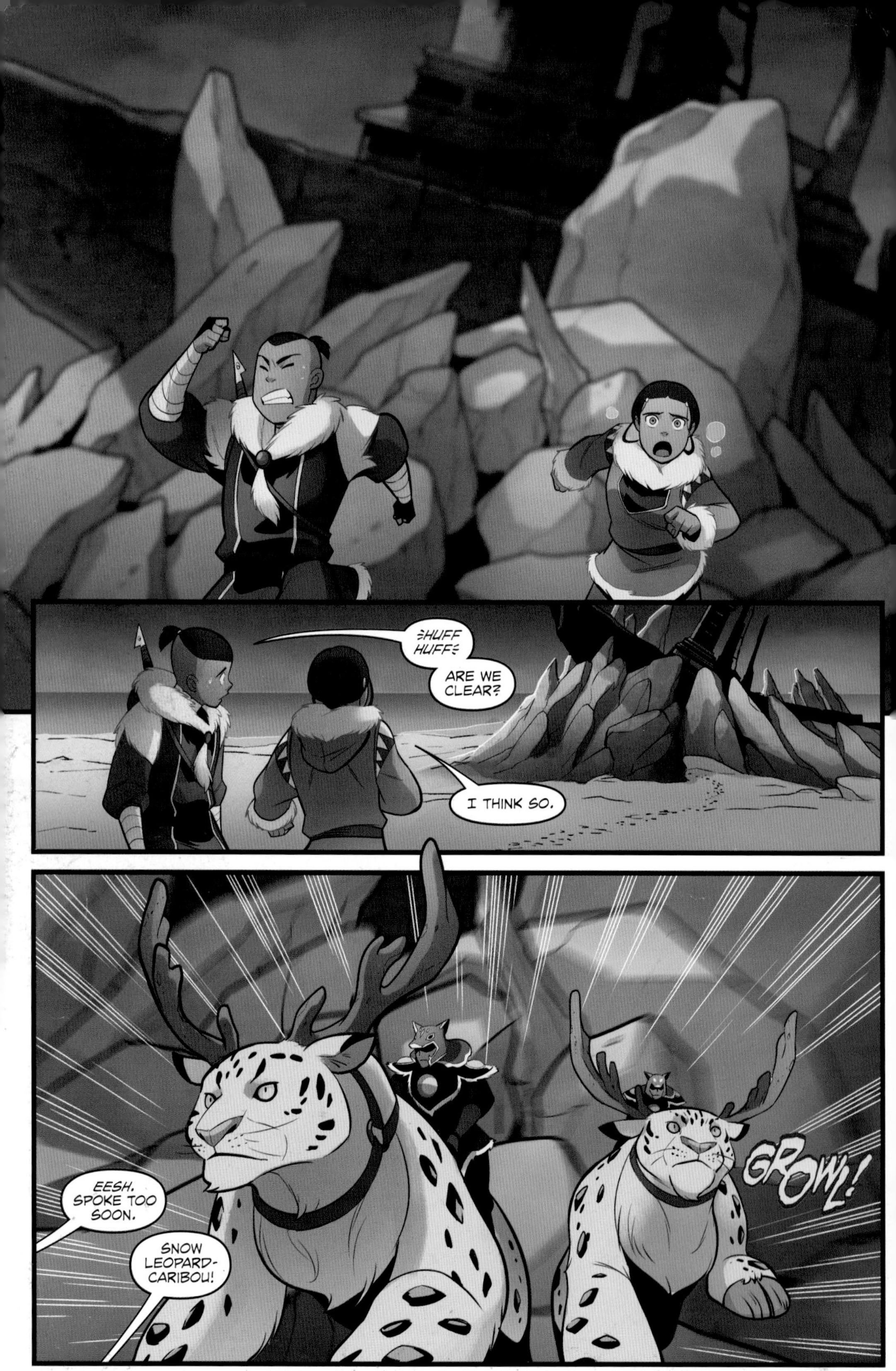
HUFF HUFF
ARE WE CLEAR?
I THINK SO.
EESH. SPOKE TOO SOON.
SNOW LEOPARD-CARIBOU!
GROWL!

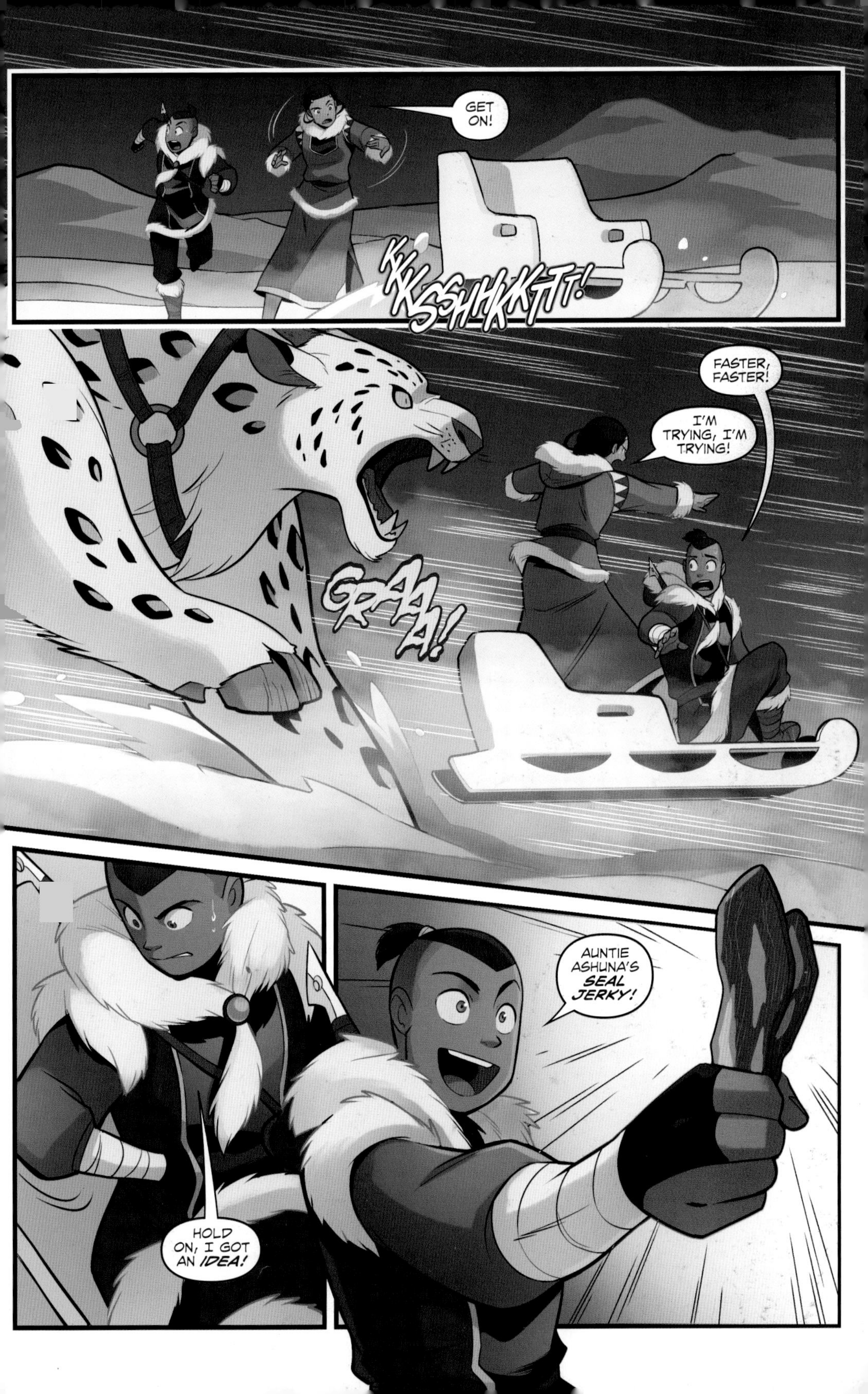
GET ON!
KKKSSHHKKTTTT!
FASTER, FASTER!
I'M TRYING, I'M TRYING!
GRAAAA!
HOLD ON, I GOT AN *IDEA!*
AUNTIE ASHUNA'S *SEAL JERKY!*

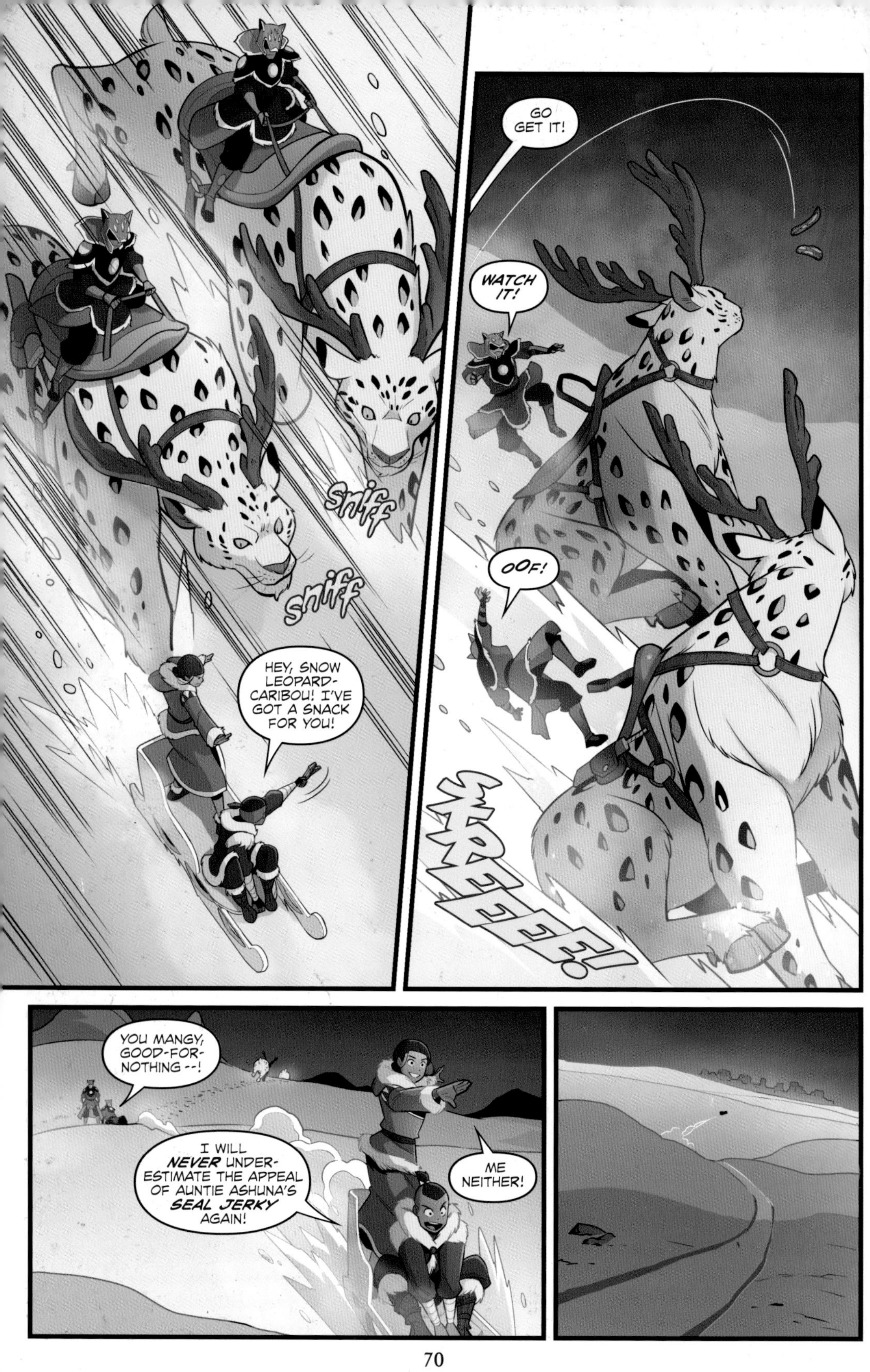

sniff
sniff
HEY, SNOW LEOPARD-CARIBOU! I'VE GOT A SNACK FOR YOU!
GO GET IT!
WATCH IT!
OOF!
YOU MANGY, GOOD-FOR-NOTHING --!
I WILL NEVER UNDER-ESTIMATE THE APPEAL OF AUNTIE ASHUNA'S SEAL JERKY AGAIN!
ME NEITHER!

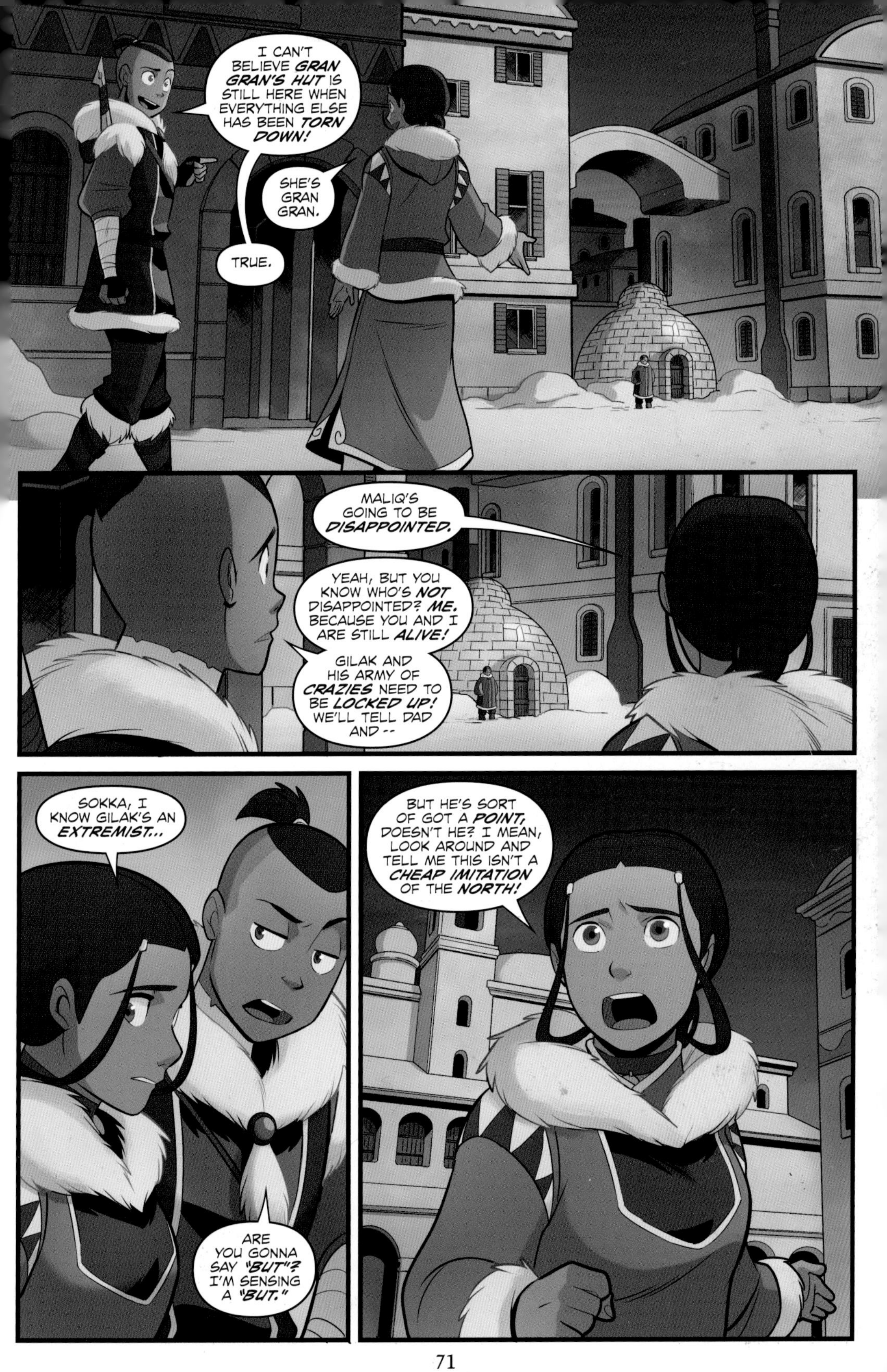
I CAN'T BELIEVE GRAN GRAN'S HUT IS STILL HERE WHEN EVERYTHING ELSE HAS BEEN TORN DOWN!
SHE'S GRAN GRAN.
TRUE.
MALIQ'S GOING TO BE DISAPPOINTED.
YEAH, BUT YOU KNOW WHO'S NOT DISAPPOINTED? ME. BECAUSE YOU AND I ARE STILL ALIVE!
GILAK AND HIS ARMY OF CRAZIES NEED TO BE LOCKED UP! WE'LL TELL DAD AND --
SOKKA, I KNOW GILAK'S AN EXTREMIST...
ARE YOU GONNA SAY "BUT"? I'M SENSING A "BUT."
BUT HE'S SORT OF GOT A POINT, DOESN'T HE? I MEAN, LOOK AROUND AND TELL ME THIS ISN'T A CHEAP IMITATION OF THE NORTH!

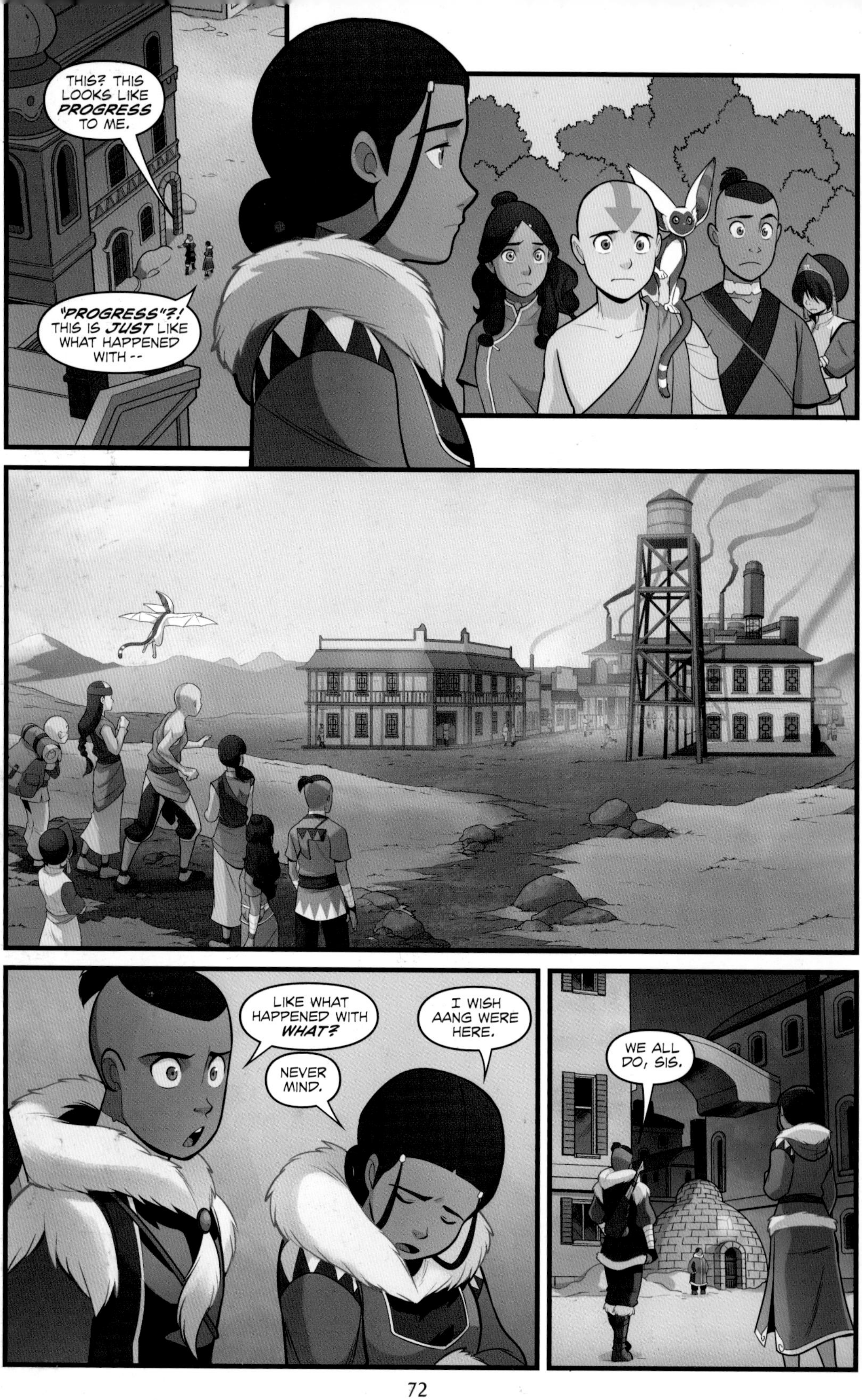
THIS? THIS LOOKS LIKE PROGRESS TO ME.
"PROGRESS"?! THIS IS JUST LIKE WHAT HAPPENED WITH --
LIKE WHAT HAPPENED WITH WHAT?
NEVER MIND.
I WISH AANG WERE HERE.
WE ALL DO, SIS.

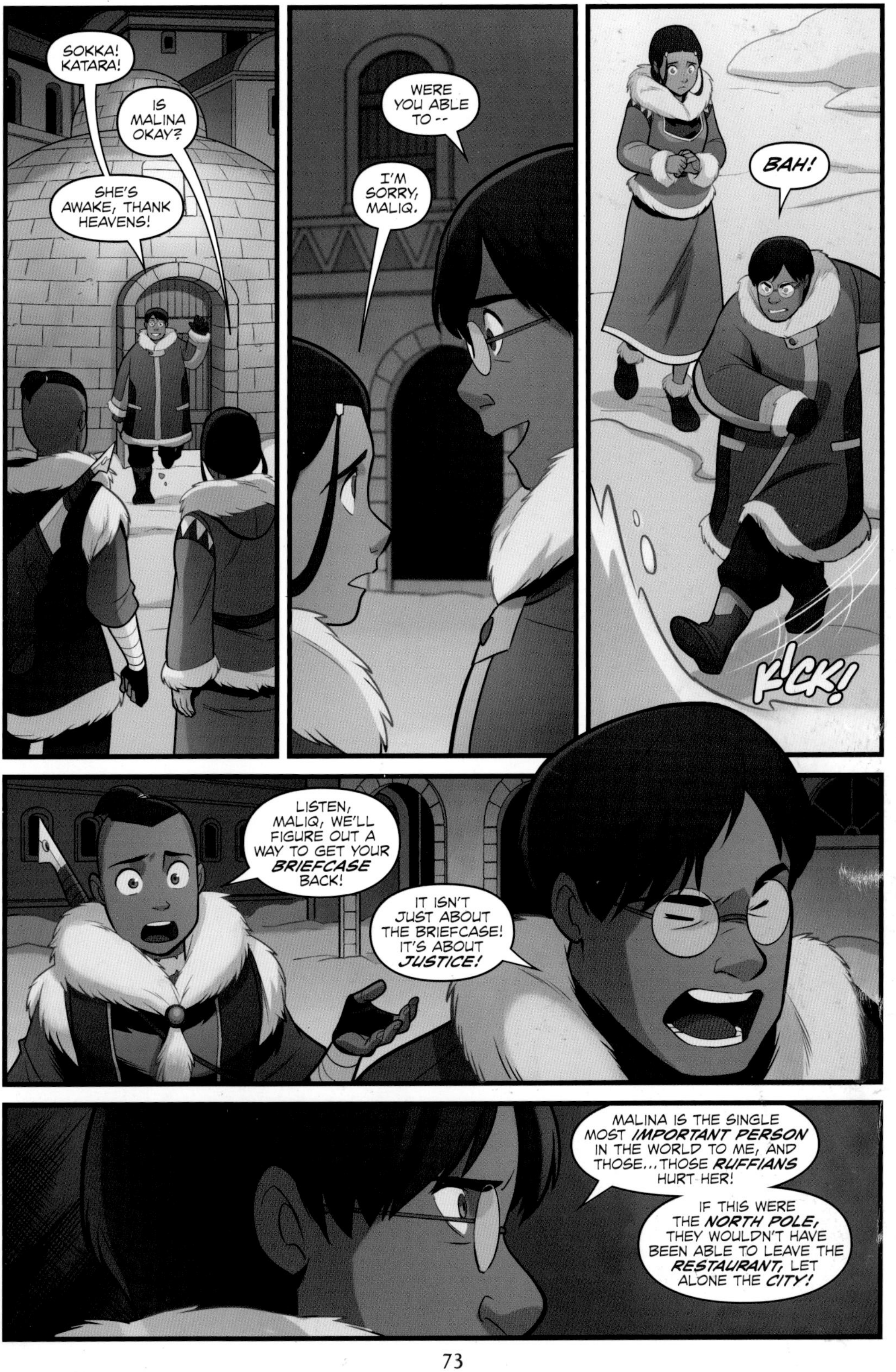
SOKKA! KATARA!
IS MALINA OKAY?
SHE'S AWAKE, THANK HEAVENS!
WERE YOU ABLE TO --
I'M SORRY, MALIQ.
BAH!
K'CK!
LISTEN, MALIQ, WE'LL FIGURE OUT A WAY TO GET YOUR BRIEFCASE BACK!
IT ISN'T JUST ABOUT THE BRIEFCASE! IT'S ABOUT JUSTICE!
MALINA IS THE SINGLE MOST IMPORTANT PERSON IN THE WORLD TO ME, AND THOSE... THOSE RUFFIANS HURT HER!
IF THIS WERE THE NORTH POLE, THEY WOULDN'T HAVE BEEN ABLE TO LEAVE THE RESTAURANT, LET ALONE THE CITY!

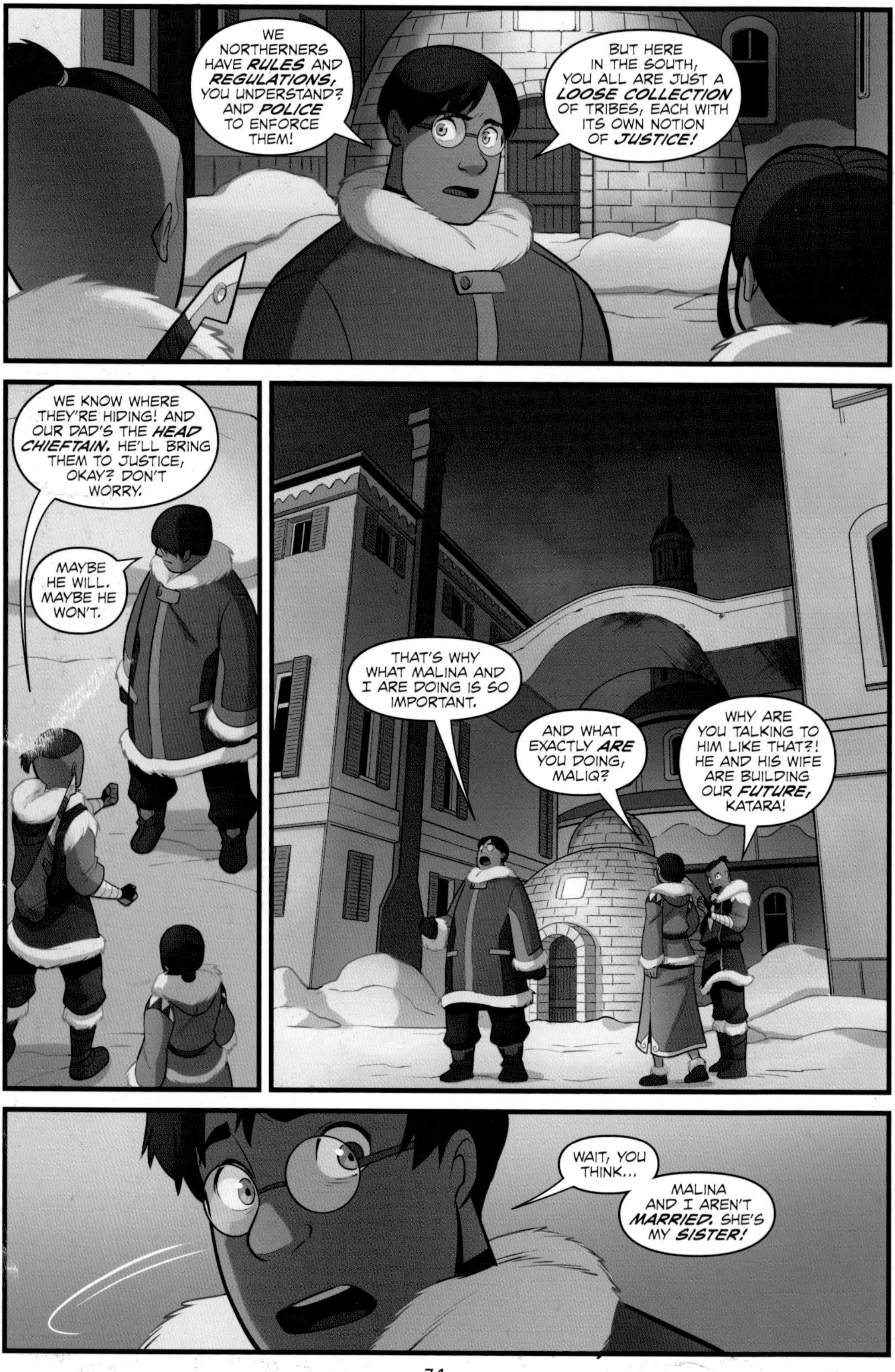
WE NORTHERNERS HAVE RULES AND REGULATIONS, YOU UNDERSTAND? AND POLICE TO ENFORCE THEM!
BUT HERE IN THE SOUTH, YOU ALL ARE JUST A LOOSE COLLECTION OF TRIBES, EACH WITH ITS OWN NOTION OF JUSTICE!
WE KNOW WHERE THEY'RE HIDING! AND OUR DAD'S THE HEAD CHIEFTAIN. HE'LL BRING THEM TO JUSTICE, OKAY? DON'T WORRY.
MAYBE HE WILL. MAYBE HE WON'T.
THAT'S WHY WHAT MALINA AND I ARE DOING IS SO IMPORTANT.
AND WHAT EXACTLY ARE YOU DOING, MALIQ?
WHY ARE YOU TALKING TO HIM LIKE THAT?! HE AND HIS WIFE ARE BUILDING OUR FUTURE, KATARA!
WAIT, YOU THINK...
MALINA AND I AREN'T MARRIED. SHE'S MY SISTER!

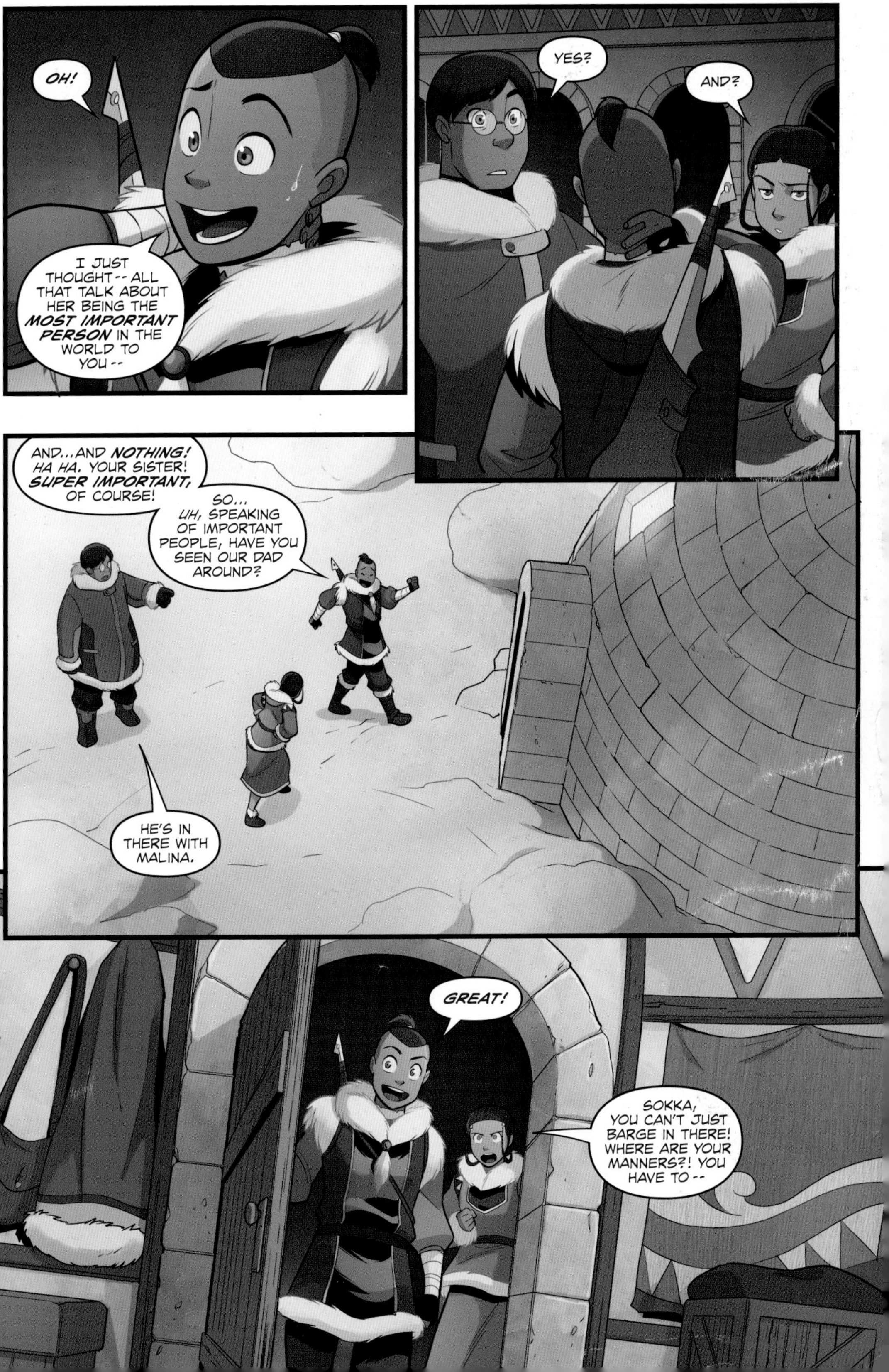

OH!
I JUST THOUGHT -- ALL THAT TALK ABOUT HER BEING THE MOST IMPORTANT PERSON IN THE WORLD TO YOU --
YES?
AND?
AND...AND NOTHING! HA HA. YOUR SISTER! SUPER IMPORTANT, OF COURSE!
SO... UH, SPEAKING OF IMPORTANT PEOPLE, HAVE YOU SEEN OUR DAD AROUND?
HE'S IN THERE WITH MALINA.
GREAT!
SOKKA, YOU CAN'T JUST BARGE IN THERE! WHERE ARE YOUR MANNERS?! YOU HAVE TO --

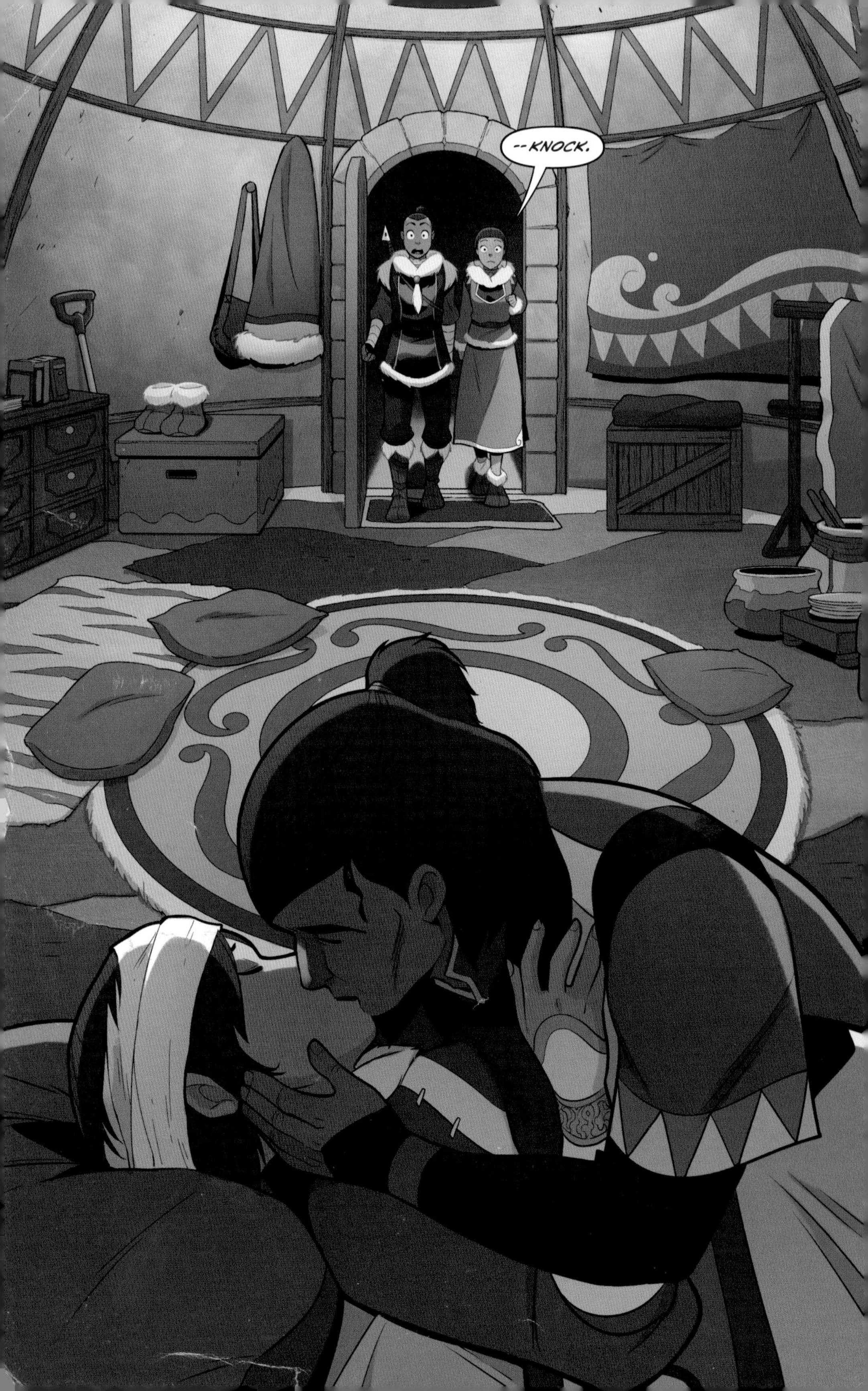
--KNOCK.

COMING IN JANUARY 2017

Team Avatar is reunited in . . .

NORTH AND SOUTH · PART TWO

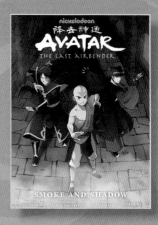

Avatar: The Last Airbender—The Promise Library Edition
978-1-61655-074-5 $39.99

Avatar: The Last Airbender—The Promise Part 1
978-1-59582-811-8 $10.99

Avatar: The Last Airbender—The Promise Part 2
978-1-59582-875-0 $10.99

Avatar: The Last Airbender—The Promise Part 3
978-1-59582-941-2 $10.99

Avatar: The Last Airbender—The Search Library Edition
978-1-61655-226-8 $39.99

Avatar: The Last Airbender—The Search Part 1
978-1-61655-054-7 $10.99

Avatar: The Last Airbender—The Search Part 2
978-1-61655-190-2 $10.99

Avatar: The Last Airbender—The Search Part 3
978-1-61655-184-1 $10.99

Avatar: The Last Airbender—The Art of the Animated Series
978-1-59582-504-9 $34.99

Avatar: The Last Airbender—The Lost Adventures
978-1-59582-748-7 $14.99

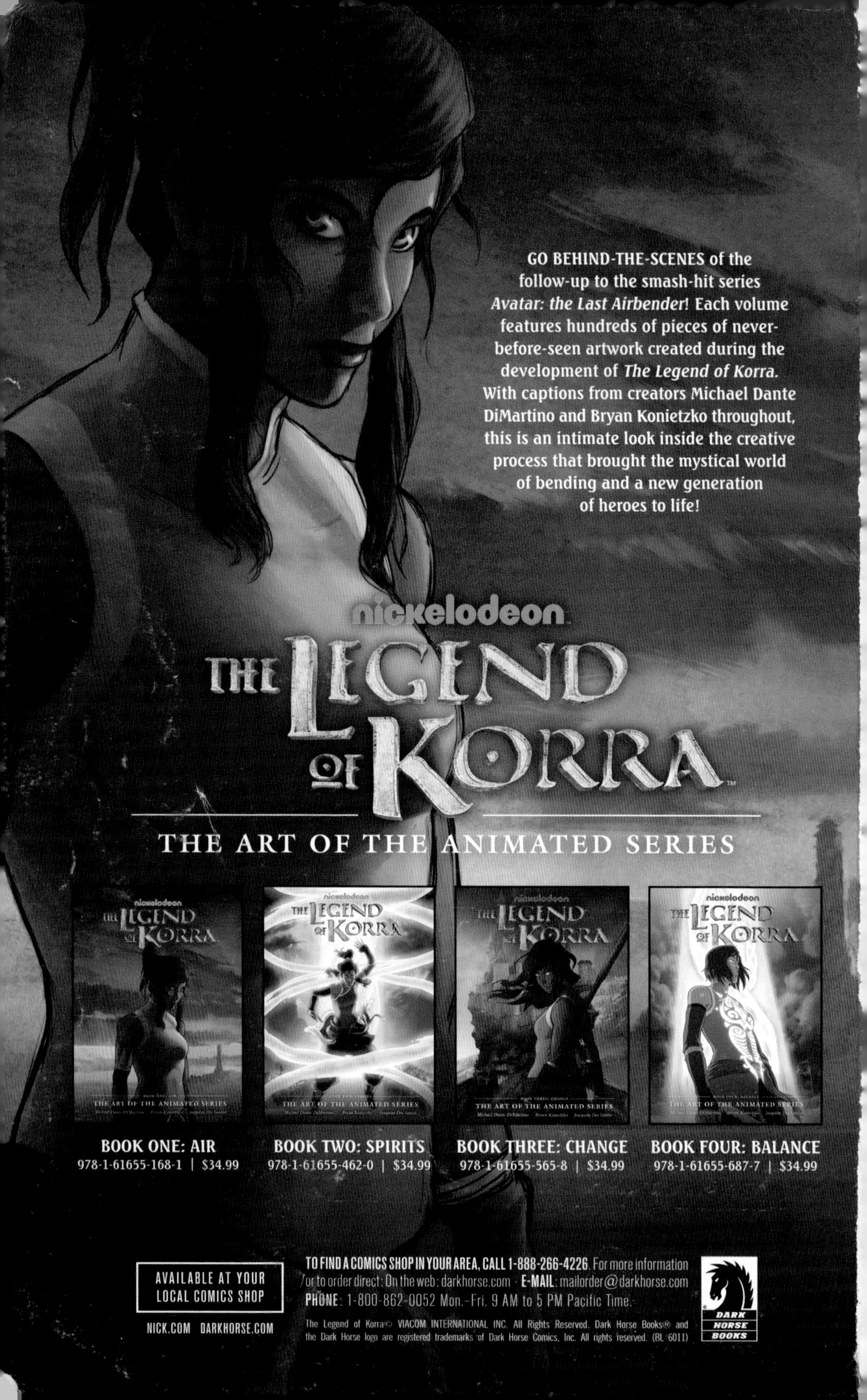
GO BEHIND-THE-SCENES of the follow-up to the smash-hit series *Avatar: the Last Airbender*! Each volume features hundreds of pieces of never-before-seen artwork created during the development of *The Legend of Korra*. With captions from creators Michael Dante DiMartino and Bryan Konietzko throughout, this is an intimate look inside the creative process that brought the mystical world of bending and a new generation of heroes to life!
nickelodeon
THE LEGEND OF KORRA™
THE ART OF THE ANIMATED SERIES
BOOK ONE: AIR
978-1-61655-168-1 | $34.99
BOOK TWO: SPIRITS
978-1-61655-462-0 | $34.99
BOOK THREE: CHANGE
978-1-61655-565-8 | $34.99
BOOK FOUR: BALANCE
978-1-61655-687-7 | $34.99
AVAILABLE AT YOUR LOCAL COMICS SHOP
NICK.COM DARKHORSE.COM
TO FIND A COMICS SHOP IN YOUR AREA, CALL 1-888-266-4226. For more information or to order direct: On the web: darkhorse.com · E-MAIL: mailorder@darkhorse.com
PHONE: 1-800-862-0052 Mon.–Fri. 9 AM to 5 PM Pacific Time.
The Legend of Korra© VIACOM INTERNATIONAL INC. All Rights Reserved. Dark Horse Books® and the Dark Horse logo are registered trademarks of Dark Horse Comics, Inc. All rights reserved. (BL 6011)
DARK HORSE BOOKS